The Evolution of
NORTH AMERICAN INDIANS

Edited by
DAVID HURST THOMAS
American Museum of Natural History

Prehistoric Warfare on the Great Plains

*Skeletal Analysis of the
Crow Creek Massacre Victims*

P. WILLEY

NEW YORK AND LONDON

First published 1990 by Garland Publishing, Inc

This edition published 2012 by Routledge

Routledge
Taylor & Francis Group
711 Third Avenue
New York, NY 10017, USA

Routledge
Taylor & Francis Group
2 Park Square
Milton Park, Abingdon
Oxfordshire OX14 4RN

First issued in paperback 2016

Routledge is an imprint of the Taylor and Francis Group, an informa business

Copyright © 1990 by P. Willey.
All rights reserved.

Library of Congress Cataloging-in-Publication Data

Willey, Patrick S.
Prehistoric warfare on the Great Plains : skeletal analysis of the Crow Creek massacre victims / P. Willey.
p. cm. — (The Evolution of North American Indians)
Based on thesis (Ph. D.)—University of Tennessee, Knoxville, 1982, originally titles Osteology of the Crow Creek massacre.
Includes bibliographical references.
ISBN 0-8240-7167-0 (alk. paper)
1. Crow Creek Site (S.D.) 2. Arikara Indians—Anthropometry. 3. Arikara Indians—Antiquities. 4. Anthropometry—South Dakota. 5. Excavations (Archaeology)—South Dakota. 6. South Dakota—Antiquities. I. Title. II. Series.
E99.A8W55   1990
978.3'58—dc20   90-48882

Design by J. Threlkeld

ISBN 13: 978-1-138-97921-5 (pbk)
ISBN 13: 978-0-8240-7167-7 (hbk)

Dedication

This work is dedicated to the *wanagi*
of the Crow Creek villagers.
I hope there are no hard feelings.

Table of Contents

Chapter	Page
Acknowledgement	xi
Abstract	xv
Preface	xvii
1990 Preface	xx
A. Introduction	xx
B. Recent Reports and Analyses	xxi
C. Crow Creek and the Reburial Issue	xxvii
D. Conclusions and Summary	xxx
1 Introduction	1
2. The Crow Creek Site and Excavations	3
3. Count and Context of the Bone Elements	8
A. Methods	10
B. Results and Discussion	14
C. Summary	35
4. Crow Creek Paleodemography	37
A. Methods and Materials	38
B. Results and Discussion	46
C. Summary	61
5. Crow Creek Cranial Affinities	64
A. Methods and Materials	65
B. Results and Discussion	74
C. Summary	90
6. Crow Creek Mutilations	93
A. Methods and Materials	95
B. Results and Discussion	105
C. Summary	149
7 . Crow Creek Stature	153
A. Methods and Materials	154
B. Results	160
C. Discussion	165
D. Summary	174
8 . Interpretation	176
A. Background	176
B. The Raid	177
C. Exposure	179
D. Burial	179
E. Excavation and Reburial	181
References Cited	183
Vita	203

List of Tables

Table		Page
1.	Elementary Articular Groups from Bed B by Age	15
2.	Minimum Element Counts of Major Bones from Crow Creek	16
3.	Crow Creek Minimum Element Counts by Age Group	18
4.	Crow Creek Maximum Element Counts for Adults and Subadults	21
5.	Maximum Counts of Crow Creek Wrist and Hand Elements Compared with Expected Numbers	22
6.	Maximum Counts of Crow Creek Ankle and Foot Elements Compared with Expected Numbers	23
7.	Crow Creek Maximum Element Count for Beds A and B	25
8.	Comparison of the Crow Creek Maximum Element Counts from Beds A and B	26
9.	Canonical Correlation Coefficients of Percentages of the Crow Creek Bed B Minimum Element Counts by Excavation Square	28
10.	Principal Component Loadings for Percentages of Crow Creek Bed B Maximum Element Counts by Excavation Square	30
11.	Canonical Correlation Coefficients of Principal Component Scores for Percentage of the Crow Creek Bed B Maximum Element Count by Excavation Square	32
12.	Pubic Symphysis Stages Assigned to Five-Year Intervals for Estimating the Adult Crow Creek Ages	42
13.	Adjusting and Smoothing the Crow Creek Age Distribution Counts	47
14.	Comparison of the Adjusted and Smoothed Crow Creek Adult Age Intervals by Sex	49
15.	Adjusted and Smoothed Age Distribution Frequencies at Crow Creek for Each Sex and Total Sample	52
16.	Smoothed Crow Creek Age Distribution Compared with the Smoothed Larson Village Sample	53
17.	Smoothed Age Distribution of Crow Creek Compared with Those of Middle Missouri Region Cemetery Samples	54
18.	Comparison of the Smoothed Age Counts of Crow Creek and Mobridge 1	55
19.	Comparison of the Smoothed Age Counts of Crow Creek and Mobridge 2	56
20.	Comparison of the Smoothed Age Counts of Crow Creek and Larson Cemetery	57
21.	Comparison of the Smoothed Cumulative Percentages of the Two Combined Massacre Samples with that of the Three Combined Cemetery Samples	58
22.	Comparison of the Smoothed Age Counts of the Two Combined Massacre Samples with that of the Three Combined Cemetery Samples	59
23.	Descriptive Statistics of Female Crow Creek Cranial Measurements	67
24.	Descriptive Statistics of Male Crow Creek Cranial Measurements	68
25.	Samples from Crow Creek Squares Combined for Analyzing Cranial Morphology Homogeneity among the Squares	70
26.	D^2 Values of Individual Crow Creek Female Crania from the Group Centroid	75

27. D^2 Values of Individual Crow Creek Male Crania from the Group Centroid ... 76
28. Hit-Miss Distribution of Female Crow Creek and Other Female Cranial Samples ... 83
29. Hit-Miss Distribution of Male Crow Creek and Other Male Cranial Samples .. 84
30. Number of Discrete Traits Absent and Present, Percent Present, and θ-Value for the Combined Sexes of Crow Creek ... 87
31. Morphological Distances Based on 16 Cranial Discrete Trait Frequencies of Crow Creek and Other Samples ... 88
32. Mutilations of Skulls from Crow Creek ... 106
33. The Location of Cuts on the Crow Creek Skulls and Skull Fragments Suggesting Scalping by Age and Sex ... 107
34. Comparison of the Crow Creek Cranial Cuts by Age ... 108
35. Comparison of Adolescent and Child Cranial Cuts from Crow Creek ... 110
36. Comparison of Female and Male Cranial Cuts from Crow Creek ... 112
37. Skulls with and without Depressed Fractures from Crow Creek ... 115
38. Location of Depressed Fractures on Crow Creek Skulls ... 116
39. Comparison of Crow Creek Decapitation Cuts by Element Including Uncertains ... 121
40. Comparison of Crow Creek Decapitation Cuts by Element Excluding Uncertains ... 122
41. Number of Crow Creek Long Bones with Cuts ... 125
42. Crow Creek Long Bone Modifications from Bed B ... 127
43. Modifications of Non-Long, Postcranial Bones from Crow Creek ... 128
44. Crow Creek Village Postcranial Modifications ... 132
45. Mutilations of Skulls from Larson Village ... 134
46. Larson Village Long Bone Modifications ... 135
47. Modifications of Non-Long, Postcranial Bones from the Larson Village ... 136
48. Approximate Dates, Femur Sample Sizes, Means, Standard Deviations, and Dimorphism of Crow Creek and Other Sites ... 157
49. Two-Way ANOVA for Arikara Femur Length, Site, and Sex ... 161
50. One-Way ANOVA's by Sex for Arikara Femur Length and Site ... 163

List of Figures

Figure		Page
1.	Map of the Crow Creek Site from Kivett and Jensen (1976:2, Fig. 1)	4
2.	Bone Bed B at Crow Creek	9
3.	Comparison of Crow Creek and Other Craniometric Samples on Canonical Variates I and II	78
4.	Comparison of Crow Creek and Other Craniometric Samples on Canonical Varieties III and IV	80
5.	Crow Creek Female and Other Female Craniometric Group Centroids Displayed on Canonical Variates I, II and III.	81
6.	Crow Creek Male and Other Male Craniometric Group Centroids Displayed on Canonical Variates I, II, and III	82
7.	Morphological Distances Based on Non-Metric Traits between Crow Creek and Other Cranial Samples	89
8.	Chewing on Left Femur Head	99
9.	Snapping of Left Humerus Shaft	101
10.	Splintering of Long Bones	102
11.	Round Depressed Fracture of Right Parietal	117
12.	Ellipsoid Depressed Fracture on Left Parietal	118
13.	Catlin's (1844, Plate 101) Illustration of Scalpings in Progress	140
14.	Relationship between Time and Arikara Femur Length by Sex	164

Acknowledgments

The data presented in this dissertation is the product of the discovery, excavation, processing, data collection and analysis of nearly 500 human skeletons. A project of this magnitude requires the assistance, cooperation, kindness, and interest of many people. The Crow Creek project included many such people at every stage of the operation.

The Crow Creek massacre project was directed by Larry Zimmerman. Tom Emerson was in-charge of the field work with Roberta Neirison, Audhild Schanche, and Ned Hanenberger doing much of the day-to-day supervising. The supervisors and the excavators endured the heat and dust of August and the penetrating cold of December as well as the omnipotent wind. Excavators were Dayton Bard, Pat Big Eagle, Audrey Blackbull, Ann Borel, Dorsey Deloria, Sid Eare, Barb Lass, Jim Sartain, Leroy "Bear" Thompson, Richard Whitten, Roger Williams, and Tom Wolf. Field work would have been impossible without the cooperation of the Crow Creek Sioux Tribal Council, the Crow Creek Sioux, the National Historic Landmark Board, Robert Alex, and Steve Ruple.

Laboratory work ran smoothly thanks to the efforts and cooperation of many workers. Mark Swegle, osteological assistant, contributed much more than his title implies; he brought expertise and exactness to the project. Jeff Buechler was the laboratory supervisor. His ability to magically materialize needed equipment, supplies, and people was amazing. His assistant, Roger Williams, contributed much support to the project, and services by Max Schmeling were invaluable. Many University of South Dakota students assisted in reconstructing the bones, organizing the data into more useable forms, and in some cases collecting data. They were Gregg Arnold, John Hoffman, Donna Jaffer, Paul Jones, Paula Mallon, Christy McGovern, Bill Nelson, Max Schmeling, Bruce Setlock, and Julie Sieh.

Steve Symes, a graduate student at the University of Tennessee, Knoxville, helped compile many of the tables dealing with mutilations.

Funding for excavation, processing, data collection, and preliminary reporting was made available by the Corps of Engineers, Omaha District (Purchase Order DACW45-78-C-0018). The reviewers of the initial draft of the preliminary report (Zimmerman et al. 1981) are thanked for the suggestions, particularly Jane E. Buikstra and M. Pamela Bumsted.

Some of the figures presented here were drawn by Terry Faulkner. The site map is from Kivett and Jensen (1976:2, fig. 1) and was kindly made available by the Nebraska State Historical Society. The Crow Creek skeletal material found in earlier excavations and housed at the Nebraska State Historical Society was made available through the assistance and efforts of Marvin F. Kivett and Gayle F. Carlson.

Useful historic resources were brought to light by Warner Granade and Deborah Thompson, reference librarians in the Hoskins Library, University of Tennessee, Knoxville. Most of the Little Big Horn Battle sources were listed by John J. Slonaker, historic reference librarian with the U.S. Army Military History Institute, Carlisle Barracks, Pennsylvania. Mildred and Waldo Wedel provided several valuable historic references and even more valuable encouragement in this project.

All members of the dissertation committee are thanked for their patience, time and understanding. William M. Bass stimulated my interest in osteology and South Dakota over 20 years ago and has continued to support me much of that period. It was his consideration and fear of flying which permitted me the chance to work on Crow Creek from the beginning of the project. Richard L. Jantz, a statistical and conceptual wizard, was always

Acknowledgements

available for consultation and perceptive enough to suggest many fruitful approaches to the data. This dissertation owes much to him. Fred H. Smith made valuable editorial comments. Edward T. Howley also provided helpful editorial comments and an humanistic perspective of the massacre.

A.J. Jaffe read a preliminary draft of the paleodemographic chapter and made valuable suggestions concerning the nature of census data.

There are several others who have also aided this effort. Doug Owsley willingly gave computer programming and statistical advice. Jack Porter provided legal advice. Marilyn Caponetti edited and typed the dissertation and Kathie Pendo typed the present version. The Anthropology Department, California State University, Chico, provided funds for printing photographs and a nice, large table for the final editing.

In addition to the assistance given by these many personal and professional friends, there are others whose influence on this project, although indirect, has been considerable. My parents instilled an interest in the macabre and encouraged the pursuit of osteology. My former wife, Stella, made graduate study emotionally tolerable and economically feasible. For more than half of a decade, Fran Tucker has provided stability and tried to instill the concept of propriety and establish a conscience. A former roommate, Warner Granade, patiently tolerated the moodiness and diarrhea which inevitably seem to accompany comprehensive examinations. Annie and Bard Selwyn taught me more about dying and living than even the hundreds of Crow Creek skeletons could. Finally, I want to thank the "guys" for extricating me from anthropological pursuits to jog, play volleyball, and drink beer, especially Steve Ruple, Anne Hawkins, Gary Scott, the Brandals, Patrick Key, Mary Allison, Warner Granade, and Steve Symes.

Abstract

About 1325 AD in south-central South Dakota nearly 500 American Indians were massacred at the Crow Creek Site. They were mutilated, exposed above ground, then buried in the fortification ditch which surrounded the Crow Creek Village. Their remains were discovered, excavated, and cleaned in 1978 and were available for study the first 5 months of 1979. The general purposes of the Crow Creek osteological study were to describe the remains as fully as time permitted and compare these results with those of other samples. This dissertation presents information concerning the Crow Creek bone elements, paleodemography, cranial affiliations, mutilations, and stature. It emphasizes the unique features of the sample and compares the Crow Creek sample with other skeletal samples from the Plains.

The major findings can be summarized as follows: At least 486 Arikara were buried, that number probably constituting roughly 60 percent of the village inhabitants. Many of the smaller, more distal and more cancellous bone elements are under-represented, and many bones show indications of chewing, snapping, and splintering. There are some indications that some of the elements were preferentially placed in the ditch although these indications are slight. There are fewer young adult females and old adult males present in the sample than expected. A number of explanations for their absence are possible, but the raiders taking captives seems a most likely explanation for the missing young women. There are many mutilations on the bones. Scalping, skull fractures, evulsions, and decapitations are common. Cranial measurements indicate the Crow Creek sample were Arikara Indians and otherwise most similar to the Pawnee and St. Helena samples. There appear to be no morphologically alien skulls in the sample and no kin-affiliated burial placement of the skulls in the fortification ditch. The Crow Creek sample was shorter than subsequent Arikara samples, but only the females were significantly shorter. Their stature may indicate dietary insufficiencies and illnesses, but additional testing of this hypothesis is necessary.

Preface

The Crow Creek Site is a large, well-preserved, prehistoric Amerindian village in central South Dakota. It is on the registry of National Historic Landmarks. In May 1978 during the annual meeting of the South Dakota Archaeological Society, the site was toured. One of the group members went to inspect the outer fortification ditch and the erosion at each end. At the northwest end of the outer ditch, where a large erosional gully had formed, he discovered human bones eroding from the bottom of the ditch about 8 feet below ground surface. The bones exposed indicated that several skeletons might be present. Steps were taken to recover the bones by a University of South Dakota crew working in the area using the funding from Omaha District of the Corps of Engineers. John B. Gregg and Willey were asked to provide osteological advice for the project. Permission was sought and granted by the Crow Creek Sioux Reservation Tribal Council, the Corps of Engineers, and the National Historic Landmark supervisors to excavate and analyze the remains.

While permission was being sought and paperwork processed, the bones at the end of the ditch were looted by a vandal using a mattock or crowbar. A hole, measuring 4.5 feet high, 6 feet wide, and 3 feet deep, was cut into the bank. Nearly 50 individuals were contained in this small volume of earth, and more bones were observed continuing into the back of the hole. The looted material was collected in July, washed and a preliminary analysis (Willey 1978) made.

Plans were made to conduct a full-scale excavation which began in August and continued into early December when weather made further digging impractical. Although more bones remained in the ditch when excavation ceased, it is believed, based on the slope of the bones, that more than 95 percent of the human material has been excavated (Emerson 1979).

Laboratory processing and preparation of the bones began at the University of South Dakota during the fall. Skeletal analysis got off to a sputtering start in November and continued at an increasing rate from January until the end of May 1979, when the bones were returned to the Crow Creek Sioux for reburial.

Reburial of the bones occurred August 10, 1981. The bones were placed in six asphalt-coated concrete crypts, and Christian and traditional ceremonies were performed. The bones were buried near the south end of the Crow Creek Village Site in an old, filled excavation pit.

Because of the short period the bones were available for study, the work conducted amounted to salvage osteology. The osteological analysis was divided initially between Gregg and Willey: namely, Gregg studying the antemortem paleopathology and Willey the rest. The approach Willey took first was to gather data comparable to that which had been gathered previously from other skeletal material from the same region. Of first priority were cranial measurements and nonmetric observations, postcranial measurements, and age and sex assessments. In addition to analyses already precedented in the region, two other approaches were emphasized. An inventory of bone elements present was performed to determine the number of individuals present and the frequency of the various elements. Also a concerted effort was made to identify perimortem trauma which might indicate cause of death or mutilation. Once these data were collected and other potentially fruitful analyses identified, additional, lower priority analyses were conducted. For the most part, these other studies occurred after Willey left South Dakota to return to Tennessee and were directed and executed by Mark Swegle. There are additional, on-going studies, including an analysis of transverse lines by Steve A. Symes and trace element analysis by M. Pamela Bumsted, not to mention the continuing study of paleopathology by Gregg.

The present study is limited to the data considered to be first priority. The title of the dissertation, *Osteology of the Crow Creek Massacre*, then, may be somewhat misleading because it does not attempt to include all the areas considered important for a thorough understanding of the Crow Creek massacre. However, it is believed that this work will form a base for other investigations.

Parts of this dissertation have appeared earlier in other places and other forms. Most of Chapter 5, "Crow Creek Cranial Affinities," and part of Chapter 3, "Count and Context of the Bone Elements," Chapter 4, "Crow Creek Paleodemography," and Chapter 6, "Crow Creek Mutilations," were published in *The Crow Creek Site (39BF11) Massacre: A Preliminary Report* (Zimmerman et al. 1981). The basis for Chapter 7, "Crow Creek Stature," was presented as "Changing Stature among the Arikara," a paper given on November 6, 1980 at the 38th Annual Plains Conference, Iowa City, Iowa. The dissertation was originally titled *Osteology of the Crow Creek Massacre* and was accepted by the University of Tennessee, Knoxville in 1982. All of these chapters and the dissertation itself have undergone considerable modifications from their original forms.

1990 PREFACE

A. Introduction

A person never recovers fully from his dissertation. A dissertation, it is said, is terminal. Now, after working on this dissertation material for more than a decade, I am beginning to believe it.

In 1978, when several of us stood at the edge of the Crow Creek Site looking at the eroded and partially looted skeletons of a fourteenth century massacre, none of us knew what joys and headaches would consequently befall us. None of us knew that we would be working with the largest archaeologically recovered massacre in the world. Several years later in 1982, after completing work on this dissertation, I naively thought that a chapter in my academic and personal life was nearly complete. It seemed certain that an editorial hero more energetic, more committed, and more motivated than I would gather the useful portions of this dissertation, collect the work of others concerning Crow Creek, publish all of those works as a whole, and all of us would continue much as before with the Crow Creek "experience" behind us. That would be that, or at least so I thought. However, before the publication could proceed, typographical errors needed to be corrected, and revisions and a few additional chapters needed completing. These changes were finished in 1985, another three years having passed. But now five years after that date, the anticipated volume on the Crow Creek massacre has not materialized, and it seems unlikely to appear, at least in the foreseeable future.

So I am delighted to have this opportunity to have the osteology of the Crow Creek massacre more widely distributed than previously possible and presented in a full-length form.

The format here is similar to that of the 1982 dissertation, but with some important exceptions. The numerous typographical errors and erroneous numbers that survived the various dissertation drafts have once again been attacked. In addition to those corrections, the changes made in the 1985 revisions to the dissertation have been included; the additional new chapters written by 1985, however, have been omitted because they deviate from the principal course of the dissertation. To update the modified dissertation, this preface presents more recent osteological studies, results, and influences, emphasizing those from the Middle Missouri Region of North and South Dakota. The greatest recent influence on human osteology, the reburial issue, is considered, stressing reburial in South Dakota. This preface also reviews the significance of the Crow Creek materials and analyses.

Having the information in the dissertation more widely disseminated will be a relief. If it is true that a person never recovers fully from his dissertation, then this publication may bring with it a period of remission.

B. Recent Reports and Analyses

Since the collection of the Crow Creek data in 1978 and 1979, its information has been used and its importance has been noted in many studies. There have also been many studies performed on other skeletal series from the Middle Missouri Region and adjacent regions, which, although not employing Crow Creek data, have had an influence on or ramifications for the interpretation of Crow Creek. There have also been recent studies which for one reason of another excluded the Crow Creek data. Such advances result from a decade of progress in osteological studies.

First, although, there are a few articles presenting the background of Crow Creek. The basic archaeological conclusions and reburial issue have been reported in summary articles by Zimmerman and Whitten (1980), Zimmerman and Alex (1981a, 1981b), and Willey (1981). Willey and Emerson (ms) are currently preparing a more technical, article-length overview using some of the same data presented in this dissertation, including some verbatim sections. Zimmerman (ms) is also preparing a manuscript presenting a model for Initial Coalescent warfare based in part on Crow Creek. These publications provide or will provide when published the background of the archaeology and osteology of Crow Creek.

Of the materials recovered from the Crow Creek excavation, the skeletons are by far the most numerous and most captivating of the discoveries. It is little wonder that analytical emphasis has been placed on them.

One of the purposes of this dissertation is to provide a basic description of this unique skeletal series. But as one dissertation committee member pointed out during the oral examinations, every description is always, by its nature, incomplete and always subject to criticisms for sins of omission. Why, he asked, if indeed this was the osteology of Crow Creek, were dental health, dental metrics, limb bone growth, postcranial discrete traits, antemortem paleopathology, trace element analysis and a host of other significant data sets excluded? Tough question.

Fortunately in the years that have passed since that question was raised, other researchers have analyzed and reported data sets other than those presented here. Gregg and co-workers (Gregg 1982, Gregg and Gregg 1979, 1987, Gregg et al. 1981, Gregg and Zimmerman 1986, Loveland et al. 1984, Zimmerman et al. 1980) have described the Crow Creek paleopathology, emphasizing the antemortem disease conditions. They found a full range of antemortem diseases in the Crow Creek skeletal series, including various congenital malformations, trauma, infectious processes, tumors, metabolic disturbances, and degenerative diseases. In a more detailed study, Symes (1983) analyzed the Harris Lines on the tibia. In addition, Crothers et al. (ms) analyzed cribra orbitalia data; they found cribra orbitalia, suggesting iron deficiency, much more frequent at Crow Creek than other sites from the region. Bumsted (1985) analyzed the stable carbon isotopes from Crow Creek bone and found a high reliance on corn in the diet with individuals having cribra orbitalia being more maize dependant that those without the lesions and females being more maize dependant than males.

More striking than the Crow Creek antemortem conditions were the indications of perimortem trauma. In 1982 the magnitude and frequency of violence at Crow Creek was thought unique in the Middle Missouri Region. While still unparalleled in magnitude, recent publications have confirmed the relatively common occurrence of violence at Middle Missouri Region sites. Shermis (1982-1984) summarizes trauma from the historic Leavenworth Site (39CO9) in north-central South Dakota; there he finds numerous indications of trauma, some that probably resulted from interpersonal violence. Rose et al. (1984:73-74), studying skeletal material from Ft. Yates, found splintered limb bones which they considered indicative of perimortem damage. Willey et al. (1987:41-42) describe a prehistoric adult male from the Vermillion Bluff Site (39CL1-15510), southeast South Dakota, with a projectile point in his scapula; there are no indications of healing. The same investigators (Willey et al. 1987:131-133) also describe an adult male from South Dakota, but otherwise lacking provenience, with iron projectile points in his humeri. And finally Owsley (1988), using a sample of over 700 skeletons from Coalescent Tradition cemeteries, found indications of scalping on as many as 15 percent of the series. It is clear that a sizeable proportion of the prehistoric, protohistoric and historic Native Americans living on the Great Plains faced endemic warfare and the possibility of deaths from interpersonal violence. Crow Creek, while especially noteworthy for its large number of victims, is just one of many indications of hostilities in the Middle Missouri Region.

Taphonomy has become more emphasized in the last decade than previously, and the Crow Creek specimens are of particular interest. They underwent an array of taphonomic processes: first there was the murder and the mutilation of the villagers, followed by scavenging and decomposition, stabilized by collecting and burying the body parts, then exposure by erosion, later looting and excavation, and completed with cleaning, analysis, and reburial. This variety of processes is rivaled at only a few other North American sites, including some of the "cannibalized" skeletal series from the Southwest (Turner 1983) and the more widely known Custer Battlefield.

Many of the same taphonomic processes that occurred at Crow Creek also occurred at the Custer Battlefield. The 1876 Custer Battlefield casualties were killed, mutilated, exposed, scavenged, decomposed, buried, exposed by erosion and scavengers, reburied, and finally exhumed and buried in a mass, secondary grave. Archaeological excavation of a small number of the primary burial locations in the mid-1980's found numerous small and fragmented bones, a few large bones, and occasional articulated elements (Scott et al. 1989). These elements, overlooked at the original burial locations during exhumation, represent the inverse of the elements recovered from the Crow Creek secondary mass grave; the skeletal elements in the Custer mass grave would be comparable in many ways to those excavated at Crow Creek. Nevertheless, the processes in effect were much the same. And understanding these similarities and differences can lead to a more accurate interpretation of both sites and the taphonomic processes involved. However, before accurate comparisons and contrasts can be made, more of the Custer Battlefield graves must be excavated.

Of the similar taphonomic processes at Crow Creek and Custer Battlefield, the one receiving the most attention is canid scavenging. Scavenging at Crow Creek has been reanalyzed by Snyder and Willey (1989), comparing it with another archaeological massacre, modern forensic cases, and deer carcasses experimentally fed to captive wolves. Omitting the deer, the Crow Creek specimens showed more canid damage and less skeletal element survival than either of the other human samples. Snyder, Galloway and Willey are now exploring the role of bone density in element survival and canid scavenging; the results of this study will be applicable to Crow Creek scavenging. Since Crow Creek's recovery, another scavenged skeleton from the Middle Missouri Region has been described, this one from Ft. Manuel (39CO5-586) in north-central South Dakota. There, the limb bones of a previously reported historic adult male(?) display chewing, most likely by a canid (Willey et al. 1987:49-51). Rare as they may be, it is apparent that scavenged human remains are present in the archaeological materials from the region and in some cases have been overlooked or misinterpreted by previous observers.

In contrast with taphonomy, relatively little on-going research has occurred using the Crow Creek paleodemography. This deficiency reflects the general de-emphasis of the topic within the region. Only a few authors have considered directly the paleodemography of the Middle Missouri Region skeletal material and only one article emphasizing demography (Jantz and Owlsey 1985) has been published since 1982. The Crow Creek age and sex estimations are comparable to those used on the other skeletal series, and the Crow Creek data may be employed in future intersite comparisons.

On the other hand, there are some Crow Creek data sets which are not comparable to the data collected by subsequent researchers. In the Middle Missouri Region, numerous osteological analyses have been performed which exclude the Crow Creek data. The growth and development of infants and children in skeletal series have been studied (Jantz and Owsley 1984a, 1984b; Owsley 1985; Owsley and Hawkinson 1981; Owsley and Jantz 1985). Because these growth studies involve single individuals with both teeth and limb bones, associations not found in the disarticulated Crow Creek series, the Crow Creek data could not contribute to these studies. Adult postcranial measurements from the Middle Missouri Region have been gathered and reported (Puskarich 1984, Zobeck 1983) since Crow Creek was analyzed. The Crow Creek postcraniometrics are more limited in the measurements taken and many measurements are not comparable to those taken in the subsequent analyses. However, one comparable measurement--maximum femur length--has been investigated subsequently (Zobeck 1983) and Zobeck's results differed from those reached in this dissertation. These differences are discussed in the body of the dissertation. Intersite craniometric analyses, long the emphasis of Plains skeletal studies, have been synthesized by Key (1983). The omission of the Crow Creek craniometrics from that synthesis because of noncomparable measurements is also discussed in the body of this dissertation. In the last decade, intrasite variability has continued to be studied (e.g. Key and Jantz 1990, Owsley et al. 1982). Intrasite craniometric variability by skull location was examined at Crow Creek and is reported in the body of this dissertation.

Now, eleven years after the first Crow Creek skeletal analyses were completed, some of the data continues to be used in contemporary studies. Some of it is being reanalyzed and amplified with auxiliary analyses. Many of the data sets, however, are not comparable to those data gathered in subsequent analyses and so Crow Creek has been omitted from these studies. As unfortunate as these losses are, these and other valuable data were lost to present and future analysts when the Crow Creek skeletons were buried in 1981. This loss is a difficulty inherent in reburial.

C. Crow Creek and the Reburial Issue

When contract negotiations in 1978 among the Crow Creek Sioux Tribe, the Corps of Engineers, and the University of South Dakota agreed to bury the Crow Creek skeletons following five months of analysis, it was apparent that only a minimal amount of information could be gathered. Much would be lost. At that time, the return of the Crow Creek skeletons was considered by some of us a worst-case scenario: namely, a unique skeletal series being hastily analyzed under stressful conditions with too little funding. To compound these problems, South Dakota at that time had one of the most restrictive reburial positions contrasted with any of the nearby states. These problems did not go unheeded.

To avoid similar situations, when the state of South Dakota formally passed legislation mandating reburial, that legislation was implemented under the Administrative Rules of South Dakota (ARSD). According to the ARSD (1986), recovered human skeletal remains must be analyzed within five years of their discovery by a qualified expert who is compensated by the state. There is also a provision for retaining skeletal materials beyond this five year time limit if the remains are from mass burials or of extreme importance. Crow Creek would qualify under either of these stipulations. It is clear that the author of the ARSD learned a number of lessons, as we all did, from the Crow Creek project. And now, in part because of the Crow Creek project, South Dakota has one of the most permissive reburial laws contrasted with those of the surrounding states. Unfortunately it appears that some well-meaning, but ignorant recent legislative steps are being taken to modify the state's reburial laws, making them inconsistent and more restrictive (Haug 1990, Zimmerman and Gregg 1989).

As a consequence of having funding for analysis and more reasonable time limits to analyze and report skeletal discoveries, marked improvements have been made. Since the Crow Creek analysis, a more thorough and systematic data gathering procedure has been implemented, following the methods and protocols established by Owsley and co-workers (Owsley et al. 1985). Standard data sets are collected by a team of specialists. Data sets gathered include dental, element, and joint surface inventories; age and sex information; dental disease, discrete traits, measurements, eruption, and abrasion; skeletal paleopathology; cranial nonmetric observations, measurements, and angles; and subadult and adult limb bone and adult pelvic measurements. These systematic, thorough analyses permit comparability of observations often impossible between the Crow Creek data and that gathered by other researchers.

These research reports have been funded not only by the state but also by federal agencies. Two reports have been executed for the state of South Dakota using the standard data sets just mentioned (Willey et al. 1987, Langdon et al. 1989), and the reported skeletons have been returned for reburial. Recovery and analysis funded by other agencies in the Middle Missouri Region have been more eclectic than those conducted by the state itself. Once the material is recovered by federal agencies, contracts have usually be awarded for analysis and reporting. At least one report has been completed successfully (Rose et al. 1984), although in another instance, analysis was underway when the contracting agency, the U.S. Corps of Engineers, Omaha District, suddenly ordered the skeletons returned without completion of the analysis or report (J. Williams, personal communication). Another arbitrary and capricious event was the Bureau of Land Management's 1989 mishandling of the sizeable protohistoric skeletal series from the Stoeser Site (39HU10) on the grounds of the Pierre Indian Learning Center. Following recovery of at least 90 skeletons and negotiations with the school's board, which permitted analysis before reburial, the skeletons were suddenly buried without even a cursory analysis. Federal procedures and policies were violated. Although in 1978 when excavations at Crow Creek were conducted, the Crow Creek situation was viewed as a worst case, it is clear that the situation now is even worse.

At least the Crow Creek material was inspected and analyzed and a contract report completed.

D. Conclusions and Summary

The importance of the Crow Creek skeletons is clear. Crow Creek is the largest archaeologically recovered skeletal massacre series in the world. Because all of the people died virtually simultaneously, they represent a living group better than cemetery samples, which reflect accretional deaths over several or many generations. Studying the Crow Creek remains is similar to examining members of a living village.

Crow Creek is also important for understanding prehistoric social relations, morphological affinities, and biological adaptation. Of particular interest are the impacts warfare had on the Crow Creek villagers, and beyond the village to the area and the region. Crow Creek is important for understanding the late prehistoric period in the Middle Missouri Region and the Great Plains.

The number of taphonomic processes that affected the Crow Creek remains are extraordinary, both for the kinds and the quantities of modifications. With the Crow Creek remains, a range of taphonomic processes can be examined and within a single process, the variety of expression can be explored. By being able to identify the processes and their affect on the Crow Creek assemblage, we are better able to understand the events that happened there and at other sites.

Finally the Crow Creek skeletal material is example of the scientific value inherent in skeletal remains. The reburial of the material in 1981 limited the kinds of insights we can have concerning these prehistoric Native Americans, but at least we were able to analyze the material and gain some knowledge from it. It is clear that the reburial issue has important ramifications for the way we will study and understand the past.

The fourteenth century Crow Creek massacre victims left a legacy which is still being pondered, studied, and interpreted. Many of the questions are simple and obvious, others are complex and cryptic, such questions as why and how were such a large number of people killed? Who were the raiders and who were the victims? What happened to the villagers who escaped the massacre? What happened to the victims' bodies? What ramifications did the slaughter have for the surviving villagers, the raiders, and the rest of the region's population and settlements? And what does Crow Creek have to tell us about the present? Some of these questions have been answered with reasonable certainty. Others remain to be answered.

Chapter 1
Introduction

In 1978 nearly 500 Indian skeletons were found in the Crow Creek Site fortification ditch in central South Dakota. Remains of men, women, children, and infants were recovered, all indications suggesting they were the fourteenth century Initial Coalescent inhabitants of the Crow Creek Village. There is conclusive evidence that the people were killed and mutilated, their bodies exposed above ground and chewed by carnivores before being buried in a mass grave (Zimmerman et al. 1981).

The massacre victims from the Crow Creek Site have important implications for skeletal analyses on the Plains and elsewhere. The Crow Creek skeletons are also very important for reconstructing lifeways during the Initial Coalescent period. There are some relatively unique features about the Crow Creek sample and a number of ways in which the Crow Creek material will contribute to our understanding of the past. The unique aspects of the material are the size, period, location, and nature of the sample.

The Crow Creek massacre is the earliest large skeletal sample from the Middle Missouri Region. The massacre dates approximately 1325 AD, preceding other large skeletal samples from the region by about 300 years. It is the only large Initial Coalescent skeletal sample. The Initial Coalescent is the earliest phase in the Middle Missouri Region identified on cultural and osteological grounds as leading to the historic Arikara tribe. The Crow Creek skeletons are, then, important in understanding the origins of the Arikara.

Crow Creek is also the southern-most large skeletal sample in the Middle Missouri Region. The closest large sample is from the Sully Site located about 100 miles up-river.

Most importantly, the Crow Creek skeletons are the remains of the largest archaeologically recovered massacre in North America, if not the world. As such, it is valuable for indicating the magnitude of aboriginal warfare and presenting a large sample of victims from which types and frequencies of perimortem trauma can be observed.

From a population perspective, the remains are nearly unique among skeletal samples because all of the Crow Creek individuals were members of the same group, and all were alive at one point in time. Most other skeletal samples come from cemeteries and almost always include several archaeologically inseparable generations. Although several generations are probably present in the Crow Creek sample, unlike cemetery samples, they are separable by age at death. In short, the Crow Creek sample is a deme: a skeletal "population" frozen in time.

This analysis takes these unique features of the Crow Creek sample into consideration, emphasizing some of the major contributions the material has to make in the areas of element taphonomy, paleodemography, mutilations, craniometric distance, and stature. Each area is considered in a separate chapter in a traditional structure; each chapter has an introduction, methods employed, results found, a pertinent discussion, and summary. All chapters are descriptive, and most are comparative as well. The final chapter summarizes the information gleaned in the chronological order which it occurred. But before proceeding to the chapters dealing with the osteological data, it is necessary to review information on the archaeological site, context, and history of the bones.

Chapter 2
The Crow Creek Site and Excavation

The Crow Creek Site (39BF11) is a National Historic Landmark located in Buffalo County, central South Dakota, 11 miles north of Chamberlain. It is on the east bank of the Missouri River, immediately north of the mouth of Crow Creek, both of which are impounded by Ft. Randall Dam and are part of Lake Francis Case Reservoir. The site was partially excavated in the 1950's and reported by Kivett and Jensen (1976). The background information concerning the site and excavations comes mostly from these authors, supplemented by Zimmerman et al. (1981).

The site is large, covering approximately 18 acres and rests on a prominent terrace (Fig. 1). The west boundary of the site is the steepest edge of the terrace which drops nearly vertically to the former Missouri River flood plain, now the lake, about 80 feet below the terrace surface. The southeast boundary is a less spectacular, but steep, bluff which drops to the old Crow Creek flood plain. The third and final boundary is formed by a well-marked, sinuous, 1250 foot-long fortification ditch. The site is in an excellent defensive position.

There are two components at the Crow Creek Site. The earlier component is from the Initial Middle Missouri Variant of the Middle Missouri Tradition and dates about 1100 to 1150 AD. The later component, the one of interest here, is from the Initial Coalescent Variant of the Coalescent Tradition. Based on radiocarbon dates, this component appears to date sometime between 1325 and 1450 AD, probably closer to the earlier date.

The remains of the Initial Coalescent component are impressive. There are at least 50 lodge depressions on the terrace. Two Initial Coalescent fortification ditches surround

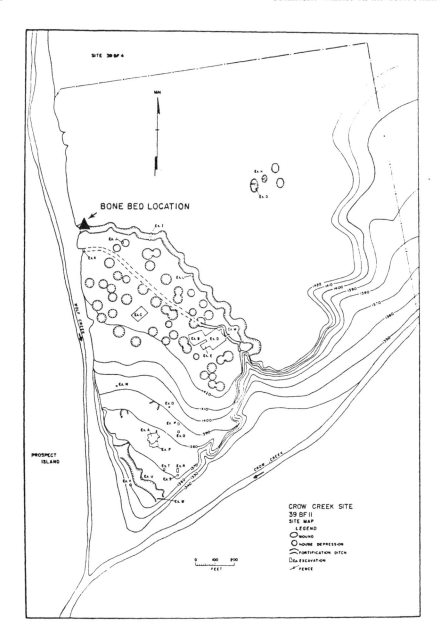

Figure 1. Map of the Crow Creek Site from Kivett and Jensen (1976:2, Fig. 1). Triangle indicates location of the bone bed.

the village on its most vulnerable side, the more prominent ditch marking the northeast and north village boundary.

The more prominent, outer ditch stretches from the Crow Creek edge of the terrace to the Missouri River side. It is 1250 feet long with 10 bristling bastions. As indicated by the single cross-section excavated, the ditch measured 6 feet deep, and more than 4 feet wide at the bottom and 12 feet wide at the top. No postholes indicating the presence of a stockade were found in a 10 by 5 foot test trench excavated on the inside of one bastion. Today the ditch is marked by a 2 or 3 foot depression and the greener, higher vegetation which grows there. It was at the extreme northwest end of this ditch where the massacre victims were discovered.

The less prominent inner ditch is visible only near the southeast corner of the village. It apparently has bastions, as the outer ditch. In contract to the outer ditch, the inner had much cultural debris plus a human mandible and cranium. These were found in the single, small excavation cross-sectioning the ditch. The inner ditch, also in contrast to the outer, has postholes, indicating an associated stockade. Six of the excavated postholes contained human skull fragments. As the outer, the inner ditch apparently dates to the Initial Coalescent occupation.

Some archaeologists have interpreted these facts as suggesting that the inner ditch was earlier than the outer ditch. As the village expanded beyond the inner ditch, according to this interpretation, it was used as a refuse dump. With increasing hostilities, fortification was again needed and so the impressive outer ditch was built to include the lodges outside the inner ditch. The skull fragments found in some of the postholes from the stockade of the inner ditch support the idea that the outer ditch had just been dug and that the stockade was being constructed in part with the posts from the inner ditch, leaving these postholes still open when the massacre happened. Evidence for this hypothesis also comes from the lack of postholes adjacent to at least part of the outer ditch and the relative lack of cultural debris in the outer ditch. In brief, the Crow Creek villagers may have been caught with their stockade down.

Formal archaeological excavations began at Crow Creek in 1954 and continued in 1955 under the direction of Marvin F. Kivett, former museum director of the Nebraska State Historical Society. Results of the excavations and analyses have been reported by Kivett and Jensen (1976). Their excavations exposed more than six structures and sectioned all of the ditches. More than 20 years after the excavations and two years after their report was published, attention was again focused on the site when human bones were discovered eroding from the outer fortification ditch in 1978. The principal logistic steps taken have been outlined in the Preface above, and additional details concerning the excavation are presented below.

Excavation of the bone bed, which is more fully described by Zimmerman et al. (1981), began with cleaning the end of the fortification ditch for inspection and superimposing a horizontal grid system over the ditch. The horizontal grid was divided into 1 meter squares, numbered in an east-west orientation and lettered north-south. Material collected was identified to the quarter of a meter square, for instance, the Northeast Quarter of Square 8B. In all, 18 meter squares or parts of meter squares (6 meters east-west, 3 meters north-south) were excavated.

Stratigraphically there were two bone beds in the deposit. Bed A was the higher and thinner of the two. Immediately above parts of Bed B was a clay and silt stratum which must have been deposited by humans because clay does not occur naturally on the terrace. The top of Bed B, the lower and much larger of the bone beds, was 1 to 2 feet below Bed A. Bed B was cone-shaped with the apex of the cone against the north wall of the fortification ditch. At the apex the bed was 4.5 feet thick. All of Bed A and the surface of Bed B were photographed and mapped. Articulated bones were given numbers and collected as units. In addition to the wealth of human bones, a few cultural and other specimens were found.

Although most of the cultural specimens from the ditch were not diagnostic, those which were (some ceramics, lithics, and a bone point) indicate all materials were from the Initial Coalescent component. There were no diagnostic Middle Missouri artifacts present.

In addition to the cultural materials in the ditch, there were some animal bones (dog?, bison, deer, and smaller mammals) and seeds of wild plants plus corn and sunflower. The over-whelming volume of material from the ditch was and the focus of this study is the human skeletal material.

Because the Crow Creek Village is so large and exceptionally well preserved and because of the attention focused on the site during excavation of the massacre victims, the site was considered for national monument status. Feasibility studies were conducted in the early 1980's, but by the end of the decade, the movement was dead. It is unlikely, despite its archaeological importance, that the Crow Creek Site will become a national monument anytime in the foreseeable future.

Chapter 3
Count and Context of the Bone Element

The huge bone pile at Crow Creek (Fig. 2) and the shelved bone-filled boxes at the University of South Dakota were alternately an osteologist's dream and nightmare. Any systematic study of the bones had to begin with an element inventory. Once the bone count was complete, more specialized studies could begin. Likewise it is appropriate to begin the osteological portion of this dissertation with information concerning the element counts.

There are two general purposes of this chapter. The first deals with the element counts and the second with the archaeological context of the elements. The purpose of the element count is to determine the number of people present as the first step in the demographic analysis, which is more fully developed in Chapter 4. The element count is also necessary for determining the proportions of the different elements present. Element proportions differing from the expected ratios may indicate dismemberment by the raiders, consumption by scavengers, or omission by the buriers.

The second general purpose of this chapter involves the archaeological context of the elements. Here, the location of the elements in the ditch and their articulation with one another are the matters of concern. The element location is analyzed based on vertical and horizontal placement. The vertical analysis is performed to see if there are differences between the superficial, overlying Bed A and the major, more deeply buried Bed B. Differences between the two bone beds may indicate different treatments or taphonomic processes. The most likely explanations for overlying Bed A is it either represents a secondary pick up of scattered elements from the massacre or it is the remains scattered by scavengers burrowing into Bed B. The horizontal analysis is performed to see if the

Count and Context of the Bone Elements 9

Figure 2. Bone Bed B at Crow Creek. More of the bone deposit remains covered at the right margin of the photograph. View is toward the north.

elements are randomly scattered through Bed B or if their position is non-random. Non-randomness may indicate special placement of certain elements or the tendency of some elements to roll down slope. The articulated elements are summarized to better understand the degree of decomposition and dismemberment of the bodies.

A. Methods

Element Count

The bone elements were counted in two ways. First an inventory of each bag was made, listing the maximum number of elements present in each bag. Because parts of the same bone may have been in two or more bags, a summation of this inventory yields a maximum count. To achieve another view of the number of elements present, a minimum count was made of the limb bones and the petrous portion of the temporal. Bones from the right and left sides were counted separately in the minimum count. Both the minimum and maximum counts were made by Mark Swegle.

Minimum counts were made of the humerus, radius, ulna, femur, tibia, fibula and the petrous portion of the temporal. For each element a single point on the bone was selected, and the count was made of these points. The points chosen for counting were selected because they were easily identified, easily sided and well preserved. Swegle believed that the points selected for counting were at least as well represented as any other points.

The following points were selected for the minimum count. The opening of the internal auditory meatus was used for the petrous portion of the temporal. The middle of the deltoid tuberosity of the humerus was counted. The base of the radial tuberosity of the radius and the base of the coronoid process of the ulna were counted. The base of the lesser trochanter of the femur was counted. The anterior crest at the level of the nutrient foramen of the tibia was selected, and the top of the triangular subcutaneous area near the distal end of the fibula was counted.

Age estimations were recorded for each element in the minimum and maximum counts. The age categories used were child (0-10 years), adolescent (11-17 years), adult ($\geq$ 18 years), subadult (0-17 years), adult or adolescent (> 11 years), and adult or subadult (> 0 years). Only these age estimations were possible at this level of analysis due to the disarticulation of the skeletons and the often fragmentary condition of the bones. Largely because of these two problems, the last three age categories listed were necessary. No sex determinations were made at this stage of the analysis.

In addition to the minimum element count, a "maximum" number of elements can be estimated. This count was made by summing the inventories made for each bag. During the inventory, bones in each bag were identified as belonging to different individuals based on repetitions of the same parts of the same elements and differences in age and sex. In this way the minimum number of elements in each bag was determined. Few attempts were made to reassemble elements in different bags so it is certain that this count in most cases is greater than an actual minimum count would have been. It is not, on the other hand, the maximum count because fragments in a bag which did not duplicate others and appeared to be the same sex and approximate age were considered to be from the same individual, although in many instances they probably represent more than one person.

Archaeological Context

The archaeological context of the bones is analyzed in three ways. The first analysis considers the vertical or stratigraphic distribution of the elements. The second analysis examines the horizontal distribution of the elements. And the third analysis considers the articulation of bones.

The stratigraphic analysis divides the maximum element count into those from Bed A and those from Bed B. All elements having an expected frequency of five or more are used in X^2 analyses. Because there are so few subadult bones from Bed A, no statistical comparison is made by skeletal age between the two beds.

To examine the horizontal distribution of both the minimum and maximum element counts, canonical correlations are executed on both counts. Both canonical correlations employ the percentage of each element from each grid square as the basic data, with the exception of the looter's hole (squares 11A, B and C). The provenience of the material from the looter's hole is inexact and not comparable with the rest of the grid system so it is omitted from these analyses. Percentages are calculated by summing all elements (maximum count) or by summing all of the seven elements of the minimum count from all squares and dividing the square sum of each element by the total count of all elements. Because the maximum count includes so many kinds of elements, a principal component analysis is performed on the percentages to reduce the number of variables. Principal component scores for each square are calculated using the percentage of each element by square, their unrotated matrix, and those components with an eigenvalue of 1.0 or greater. The principal component scores for each square are used in subsequent statistical manipulations of the maximum element count data. The canonical correlation of the minimum count uses the raw percentages of the elements by square. Then, using either the raw percentages or the principal component scores and the squares' north-south and east-west axes as location variables, canonical correlations are calculated for both minimum and maximum counts. All squares are included in the analyses except the material from the looter's hole. Both the principal component (FACTOR) and canonical correlation (CANCORR) routines are performed using SAS (SAS Institute 1979).

The third analysis concerns the articulated units found in the field. An articulated unit consists of two or more bones juxtaposed in the same position they take in the living body. Most of the more than 700 articulated units were identified and numbered in the field. Although some articulated units are not assigned numbers in the field, they were separated in the field and their apparent association noted in the laboratory. These laboratory-noted articulated units are included in this analysis.

Because an articulated unit could consist of two bones or more than 50 bones, the units were classified into elementary articular groups for analytical purposes. An elementary articular group is an articulation between two bones or two groups of bones. For instance, a head consists of two elements--a skull and mandible. A single articulation might, however, consist of several elementary articular groups; for example, a skull, mandible, and first two cervical vertebrae. This articulated unit is classified as the following elementary articular groups: head (skull-mandible), skull-neck (skull and first cervical) and neck (cervical vertebrae). With the exceptions of the skull and first cervical (C-1), and the seventh cervical (C-7) and first thoracic (T-1) elementary articular groups, the association of two or more cervicals is noted as just one elementary articular group. For instance, an articulation containing C-1 through C-7 is considered a single elementary articular group (the neck). The same approach is used with the thoracic and lumbar vertebrae; only when the first or the last vertebra is associated with an adjacent vertebral unit is a separate elementary articular group recorded. Thus, neck-midback (C-7 and T-1), midback-lower back (twelfth thoracic [T-12] and first lumbar [L-1]) and lower back-sacrum (fifth lumbar [L-5] and sacrum) are included as elementary articular groups. Likewise, no attempt is made to count each wrist, wrist-hand, hand, ankle, ankle-foot or foot articulation as an elementary articular group. For a complete list of the elementary articular groups used, see Table 1.

B. Results and Discussion

Element Count

The greatest minimum count, 486, from the right temporal (Table 2) indicates that at least 486 individuals and probably more are represented in the sample taken from the ditch.

At the other extreme, the least minimum count is the 91 left (115 right) radii. The differences between the counts of the various elements appears to be a function of size, density and proximity to the torso. In general the larger, denser bones closer to the torso are more frequently present that the smaller, lighter, more distal ones. The proximal limb elements are more fully represented than their distal counterparts; the humerus is more common ($n \geq 213$) than the ulna ($n \geq 131$) or the radius ($n \geq 115$), and the femur ($n \geq 367$) is more common than the tibia ($n \geq 269$) or the fibula ($n \geq 156$).

Count and Context of the Bone Elements 15

Table 1. Elementary articular groups from Bed B by age. Minimum numbers of individuals are in parentheses.

Articular Groups	Adult		Adolescent		Infant or Child		Subadult		Total	
Head (Skull-mandible)	128	(128)	15	(15)	24	(24)	0		167	(167)
Skull-neck (Skull-C-1)	126	(126)	13	(13)	24	(24)	3	(3)	166	(166)
Neck (Cervical vertebrae)	118		6		16		2		142	
Neck-midback (C-7 and T-1)	56	(56)	0		3	(3)	1	(1)	60	(60)
Midback (Thoracic vertebrae)	204		2		5		4		215	
Midback-lower back (T-12 and L-1)	138	(138)	1		0		3	(3)	142	(142)
Lower back (Lumbar vertebrae)	196		2		1		2		201	
Lower back-sacrum (L-5-sacrum)	135	(135)	1	(1)	1	(1)	0		137	(137)
Shoulder (Scapula-humerus)	8	(4)	1		0		0		9	(5)
Arm (Humerus-ulna or -radius)	30	(15)	1	(1)	0		0		31	(16)
Lower arm (Ulna-radius)	52	(26)	1	(1)	0		0		53	(27)
Lower arm-wrist (Ulna- or radius-carpal)	2		0		0		0		2	
Wrist (Carpals)	4		0		0		0		4	
Wrist-hand (Carpal-metacarpal)	3		0		0		0		3	
Hand (Metacarpals and/or phalanges)	3		0		0		0		3	
Pelvis (Sacrum-innominate)	55		0		1		0		56	
Hip (Innominate-femur)	94	(47)	4	(2)	3	(2)	0		101	(51)
Knee (Femur-patella)	7	(4)	0		0		0		7	(4)
Leg (Femur-tibia)	56	(28)	3	(2)	0		0		59	(30)
Lower leg (Tibia-fibula)	122	(62)	5	(3)	1	(1)	0		128	(66)
Lower leg-ankle (Tibia-tarsal)	25	(13)	1	(1)	0		0		26	(14)
Ankle (Tarsals)	29		1		0		0		30	
Ankle-foot (Tarsal-metatarsal)	22		0		0		0		22	
Foot (Metatarsals and/or phalanges)	20		0		0		0		20	
Total	1633		57		79		15		1784	
Combination of 2 or more elementary groups	372		15		19		4		410	

Table 2. Minimum element counts of major bones from Crow Creek.

Bone	Left	Right	Right Minus Left
Temporals	477	486	9
Humeri	200	213	13
Ulnae	113	131	18
Radii	91	115	24
Femora	367	367	0
Tibiae	262	269	7
Fibulae	156	143	-13

It is also noteworthy that the minimum count for all elements except the fibula is at least as great for the right side as that for the left. Because the larger, denser bones are more numerous, we might expect the absolute differences between their side counts to be greater than those of the smaller, lighter bones. But this expected difference is just the opposite of the actual side difference (Table 2). The side difference is greater in the lighter bones (radius side difference 24) than in the larger, denser bones (femur difference 0). An alternative explanation is that as the greater numbers of the larger, denser elements indicate, they were more likely to survive and be recovered than the smaller, lighter elements. And the larger, denser bones being more likely to be recovered, their frequency of each side is more similar than the frequency of the sides for the smaller bones.

Now turning to the minimum element count by age, the major discrepancy between the counts of the temporals and the long bones is in the number and proportion of children represented (Table 3). The adult elements are represented more completely than the other age groups. As an example, the least frequently represented adult element, the right radius (n = 105), is 35.8 percent of the most frequently represented adult element, the right femur (n = 293). On the other hand, the least frequently represented child elements, the left fibula, right ulna, and right radius (all n = 1), is only 0.76 percent of the most frequently represented child element, the left temporal (n = 132). Several causes may account for these differences. The higher proportion of adult long bones might have been caused by more destruction and scattering of the younger, smaller bodies by scavengers or by differential selection of larger bodies and body parts for burial. After burial, greater fragmentation of the younger and smaller long bones may have also occurred. The greater

Table 3. Crow Creek minimum element counts by age group. Numbers in parentheses are percentages by that element.

Elements	Children 0-10	Adolescents 11-17	Subadults 0-17	Adults or Adolescents >11	Adults >18	Adults or Subadults	Total
Right temporal	128 (26.3)	40 (8.2)	29 (6.0)	50 (10.3)	237 (48.8)	2 (0.4)	486
Left temporal	132 (27.7)	36 (7.5)	19 (4.0)	10 (2.1)	277 (58.1)	3 (0.6)	477
Left femur	35 (9.5)	41 (11.2)	7 (1.9)	2 (0.5)	282 (76.8)	0	367
Right femur	30 (8.2)	37 (10.0)	7 (1.9)	0	293 (79.8)	0	367
Right tibia	11 (4.1)	27 (1.0)	4 (1.5)	3 (1.1)	224 (83.3)	0	269
Right humerus	11 (5.2)	20 (9.4)	1 (0.5)	9 (4.2)	172 (80.8)	0	213
Left fibula	1 (0.6)	4 (2.6)	3 (1.9)	1 (0.6)	147 (94.2)	0	156
Right ulna	1 (0.8)	4 (3.1)	1 (0.8)	2 (1.5)	123 (93.9)	0	131
Right radius	1 (0.9)	5 (4.3)	0	4 (3.5)	105 (91.3)	0	115

number of adult femora compared to adult temporals could be explained mostly by the large number of temporals included in the adult-or-adolescent category. Isolated temporals often had to be placed in this category, especially when associated jaws were absent. Few femora, however, were placed in this category; if all observable epiphyses were fused, the bone was considered adult. This may have resulted in some adolescent femora being misidentified as adult femora. Additional factors that might have had some affect on the discrepancies are the looter's activities and the presence of some unexcavated bones that still remain in the fortification ditch. An increase in the minimum count based on comparisons of the age groupings appears to be unjustified, primarily because of the unavoidable imprecision of the age estimations.

It would have been worthwhile to do a minimum count of all elements in addition to the seven which were actually counted. Unfortunately, time and available resources made this approach unfeasible. As a consequence, the maximum element inventory count has to be used for other analyses. The analyses performed with the maximum count are the elements present, differences in the two beds, and differences in the horizontal element distribution through Bed B. We begin with the elements represented in the maximum count; the other two follow in the Archaeological Context section.

Before considering the results from using the maximum count, however, some of the limitations of that count should be noted. It is likely that the maximum counts of the large and fragile bones are higher than the actual number present. Intuitively it seems likely that the innominates, sacra, vertebrae, scapulae, sterna and to an extent, the clavicles are over-represented by this "maximum" count. It is not possible to determine how excessive the count is.

On the other hand, there are some maximum element counts which are probably fairly accurate. These counts are those of small and durable bones: the carpals, metacarpals, phalanges, patellae, coccyges, tarsals and metatarsals. With these limitations in mind, the maximum count remains the only means of inspecting the relative presence and absence of all elements, and so it is used for those analyses mentioned above, including a basic element count.

Inspecting Table 4, the impression is that generally the torso (vertebral column and hips) is better represented than most of the other parts. The elements seem to become less and less frequent the more distally they occur, but element size and density are also factors which complicate this generalization. The smaller, less dense bones were less frequently recovered than the larger, more dense ones. The same generalizations concerning size, density and proximity to the torso can also be made for the hands (Table 5) and the feet (Table 6) when these are considered separately. These results are similar to those found in the minimum count.

There are five taphonomic factors which may have influenced the element frequencies observed. Elements may have been 1) lost due to mutilation and dismemberment by the raiding group, 2) destroyed by scavengers, 3) overlooked when the body parts were picked up for burial, 4) differentially preserved, or 5) lost during excavation, processing or inspection procedures. Differential preservation is probably not an important consideration because all the bones present were well preserved. And the marked under-representation

Count and Context of the Bone Elements 21

Table 4. Crow Creek maximum element counts for adults and subadults. Elements from Beds A and B are combined. Skull fragments are omitted. Percentage of expected individuals is based on 476 adults, 144 subadults, 578 total.

Elements	Number of Elements			Number/ Individual	Minimum No. of Individuals			Percentage of Expected		
	Adult	Subadult	Total		Adult	Subadult	Total	Adult	Subadult	Total
Innominate	952	203	1155	2	476	102	578	100.0	70.8	100.0
Mandible	309	144	453	1	309	144	453	64.9	100.0	78.4
Femur	706	200	906	2	353	100	453	74.2	69.4	78.4
Sacrum	347	58	405	1	347	58	405	72.9	40.3	70.1
Lumbar vertebrae	1498	173	1671	5	300	35	335	63.0	24.3	58.0
Tibia	505	90	595	2	253	45	298	53.2	31.3	51.6
Thoracic vertebrae	3132	304	3436	12	261	26	287	54.8	18.1	49.7
Scapula	453	56	509	2	227	28	255	47.7	19.4	44.1
Fibula	426	51	477	2	213	26	239	44.7	18.1	41.3
Cervical vertebrae	1318	290	1608	7	189	42	231	39.7	29.2	40.0
Humerus	393	82	475	2	197	41	224	41.4	28.5	38.8
Ulna	251	17	268	2	126	9	135	26.5	6.3	23.8
Radius	234	21	255	2	117	11	128	24.6	7.6	22.1
Ribs	2505	260	2765	24	105	11	116	22.1	7.6	20.1
Clavicle	197	31	228	2	99	16	115	20.8	11.1	19.9
Tarsals	548	10	558	7	79	2	81	16.6	1.4	14.0
Metatarsals	294	3	297	5	59	1	60	12.4	0.7	10.4
Sternum	44	10	54	1	44	10	54	9.2	6.9	9.3
Patella	38	2	40	2	19	1	20	4.0	0.7	3.5
Carpals	93	1	94	8	12	1	13	2.5	0.7	2.2
Coccygeal vertebrae	46	0	46	4	12	0	12	2.5	0.0	2.1
Metacarpals	51	1	52	5	11	1	12	2.3	0.7	2.1
Hand phalanges	44	0	44	14	4	0	4	0.8	0.0	0.7
Foot phalanges	11	1	12	14	1	1	2	0.2	0.7	0.3

Table 5. Maximum counts of Crow Creek wrist and hand elements compared with expected numbers. This count excludes two carpals which were not more specifically identified. Expected number of individuals is based on 486 right petrous portions of temporal.

Bone	Number Observed	Number Expected	% of Expected Observed
Naviculars	20	972	2.1
Capitates	16	972	1.6
Lunates	14	972	1.4
Triquetrals	13	972	1.3
Hamates	11	972	1.1
Metacarpals	47	4860	1.0
Greater multangulars	9	972	0.9
Lesser multangulars	9	972	0.9
Proximal row phalanges	28	4860	0.6
Pisiforms	5	972	0.5
Middle row phalanges	10	3888	0.3
Distal row phalanges	0	4860	0.0

Table 6. Maximum counts of Crow Creek ankle and foot elements compared with expected numbers. This count excludes two tarsals which were not more specifically identified. Expected number of individuals is based on 486 right petrous portions of the temporal.

Bone	Observed	Expected	% of Expected Observed
Tali	146	972	15.0
Calcanea	108	972	11.1
Naviculars	71	972	7.3
Third cuneiforms	70	972	7.2
Cuboids	69	972	7.1
First cuneiforms	58	972	6.0
Second cuneiforms	53	972	5.5
Metatarsals	264	4860	5.4
Proximal row phalanges	9	4860	0.2
Distal row phalanges	2	4860	0.0
Middle row phalanges	0	3888	0.0

of the bones of the hands and feet cannot be due solely to loss during excavation, processing and inspection. The events of the raid and between the raid and the burial of the victims probably played the largest role in determining the frequencies observed. These processes include loss of bones caused by mutilation and dismemberment, loss caused by scavenging, and the omission of some of the body parts while being gathered for burial in the fortification ditch.

Archaeological Context

There are statistically significant differences between the maximum element counts in Beds A and B. The maximum element counts by beds are presented in Table 7. All elements whose expected frequency is five or greater are included in the X^2 test (Table 8). The distribution is significant ($X^2 = 150.95$, DF = 9, P < 0.001). The over-representation of skull parts and under-representation of cervical and thoracic vertebrae in Bed A and the reverse representations in Bed B appear to contribute most to the difference.

Proportionately more skull fragments than any other parts are included in Bed A. Assuming that Bed A represents a second, subsequent pick-up of bones and a second burial, the relative frequency of skull fragments might be understandable because skull parts were infrequently chewed or consumed by scavengers and are fairly easily identified. The relative absence of mandibles, femora and some other large, durable bones is more difficult to understand. Some of the meatier bones, such as femora, may have been chewed and splintered by the scavengers and less frequently recovered for burial. But the absence of other elements, especially mandibles, is difficult to explain in this manner. These

Table 7. Crow Creek maximum element count for Beds A and B. Adults and subadults are combined, although categories consisting of both adults and subadults are omitted.

Elements	Bed A Number	Bed A Percentage	Bed B Number	Bed B Percentage
Skull	55	31.4	1097	6.3
Mandible	2	1.1	451	2.6
Cervical vertebrae	7	4.0	1601	9.2
Thoracic vertebrae	22	12.6	3414	19.6
Lumbar vertebrae	15	8.6	1656	9.5
Coccygeal vertebrae	0	0.0	46	0.3
Sacrum	2	1.1	403	2.3
Scapula	1	0.6	508	2.9
Clavicle	0	0.0	228	1.3
Sternum	0	0.0	54	0.3
Ribs	25	14.3	2740	15.8
Humerus	4	2.3	471	2.7
Radius	1	0.6	254	1.5
Ulna	0	0.0	268	1.5
Carpals	1	0.6	93	0.5
Metacarpals	1	0.6	51	0.3
Hand phalanges	0	0.0	44	0.3
Innominate	12	6.9	1143	6.6
Femur	0	0.0	906	5.2
Patella	0	0.0	40	0.2
Tibia	8	4.6	587	3.4
Fibula	8	4.6	469	2.7
Tarsals	6	3.4	552	3.2
Metatarsals	5	2.9	292	1.7
Foot phalanges	0	0.0	12	0.1
Total	175	100.2	17,380	100.0

Table 8. Comparison of the Crow Creek maximum element counts from Beds A and B. Only those elements with expected frequencies of 5 or greater are included.

Elements	Bed A		Bed B	
	Expected	Observed	Expected	Observed
Skull	13.4	55	1138.6	1097
Humerus	5.5	4	469.5	471
Cervicals	18.8	7	1589.2	1601
Thoracics	40.1	22	3395.9	3414
Lumbars	19.5	15	1651.5	1656
Ribs	32.2	25	2732.8	2740
Innominate	13.5	12	1141.5	1143
Tibia	6.9	8	588.1	587
Fibula	5.6	8	471.4	469
Tarsals	6.5	6	551.5	552

$X^2 = 150.95$, DF = 9, P < 0.001

observations can also be used to support an alternate explanation that Bed A is the scattered remains left by scavengers as they burrowed into Bed B and dragged bones to the surface, our Bed A. If more bones had been recovered from Bed A, a more definitive assessment of its origin could be made.

Having considered the vertical distribution of the elements, it is appropriate to examine the results of the horizontal analysis for Bed B. The horizontal distribution of elements is examined using the percentages of the minimum and maximum element counts by grid squares.

Neither of the canonical correlations using the minimum element percentages by square grid is statistically significant at the 0.05 level, although the first one approaches significance. These results are presented below.

	Canonical Correlation	R-Squared	F-Value	DF	Probability
1	0.80268	0.64430	2.0356	14	0.0784
2	0.76072	0.57870	2.2893	6	0.1184
Wilks' Lambda Value = 0.14986, F = 2.03556, DF = 14, P = 0.07843.					

Because the relationship approaches significance and because there are similarities and differences between these results and those of the maximum count, results of the minimum count correlations are presented (Table 9) and the first canonical correlation is considered. According to the canonical correlation results, the largest positive coefficients are the humerus and the ulna. These elements tend to be more frequent in the southwest squares and less frequent in the northeast squares. These elements are contrasted with the temporal

Table 9. Canonical correlation coefficients of percentages of the Crow Creek Bed B minimum element counts by excavation square.

Variables	V1	V2
Standardized Canonical Coefficients for the Elements		
Temporal	-1.49591	-0.53527
Humerus	0.55710	1.00451
Ulna	0.85831	0.95073
Radius	-0.90157	-0.49749
Femur	0.23486	-0.92322
Tibia	-0.25523	0.05311
Fibula	0.12054	0.70507
Standardized Coefficients for the Spatial Variables		
East-west	0.70402	0.71018
North-south	0.71018	-0.70402

and radius which have large negative loadings. The temporal and radius are more frequent in the northwest squares, less frequent in the southwest squares.

The other horizontal analysis uses the maximum element count converted to percentages. It will also be recalled that these percentages were used in a principal component (PC) analysis to collapse the element information into orthogonal vectors; then a canonical correlation was executed using the principal component scores for each square and the grid system. In the paragraphs which follow, the PC's are described, then the canonical correlation results are presented.

Three PC's are extracted from the frequencies of the maximum element counts by square (Table 10). These three PC's explain 91.9 percent of the variation.

PC I has high positive loadings on virtually all elements, with only four elements having loadings less than 0.8. The elements with low loadings are some of the least common bones. This PC appears to be reflecting the varying depths of the sloped bone deposit. Squares with a large number of one element tend to be the same square with large numbers of other elements. PC I has a variance of 20.08 or 80.3 percent of the total variance.

PC II has high positive loadings on the bones of the hand and wrist as well as the coccyx and low positive or negative loadings on the others. PC II seems to emphasize many of the elements not emphasized by PC I. It has a variance of 1.86 or 7.4 percent of the total variance.

PC III has high positive loadings on the elements of the head and neck and high negative loadings on the ankle and foot elements. As PC II, PC III emphasizes some of the elements (the ankle and foot) not emphasized by PC I, but unlike PC II, PC III contrasts

Table 10. Principal component loadings for percentages of Crow Creek Bed B maximum element counts by excavation square.

Elements	PC I	PC II	PC III
Skull	0.87826	-0.22065	0.36900
Mandible	0.85763	-0.19902	0.37445
Cervicals	0.93010	-0.20090	0.23985
Thoracics	0.97519	-0.11059	0.04803
Lumbars	0.98092	-0.14768	0.03869
Coccyx	0.65290	0.30351	0.18992
Sacrum	0.98369	-0.02530	0.04375
Scapula	0.95972	0.16646	0.08953
Clavicle	0.96582	-0.01034	0.01055
Sternum	0.83581	0.29090	0.19563
Ribs	0.97535	-0.09976	0.10297
Humerus	0.98457	-0.02215	-0.07891
Radius	0.92552	-0.20694	-0.14540
Ulna	0.93466	-0.20029	-0.14394
Carpals	0.88176	0.36866	-0.17877
Metacarpals	0.73300	0.59883	-0.07903
Hand Phalanges	0.48786	0.84096	0.05474
Innominate	0.96538	-0.01089	0.19599
Femur	0.97057	-0.08407	0.03199
Patella	0.88962	0.13862	0.05119
Tibia	0.96967	-0.11801	-0.13237
Fibula	0.95886	-0.12949	-0.17675
Tarsals	0.89874	-0.16337	-0.27065
Metatarsals	0.83478	-0.28116	-0.37504
Foot Phalanges	0.78579	0.19132	-0.45326

these elements with others, in this case the bones of the head and neck. PC III has a variance of 1.03 or 4.1 percent of the total variance.

Now turning to the canonical correlation of the principal component scores by excavation square, the first of the two roots extracted is statistically significant, but the second is not. These results are presented below.

	Canonical Correlation	R-Squared	F	DF	Probability
1	0.78779	0.62061	4.0273	6	0.0041
2	0.37993	0.14434	1.4339	2	0.2658
Wilks' Lambda Value = 0.32463, F = 4.02729, DF = 6, P = 0.00408.					

The PC's contributing most to the significance (Table 11) in descending order of importance are PC II with a positive loading and PC I with a negative loading. PC III has a negative loading but contributes much less than the other PC's. The first canonical coefficient for PC I indicates there are more elements in the maximum count toward the northeast squares and fewer toward the southwest. The PC II coefficient indicates that there are more wrist, hand, and coccyx bones toward the southwest squares and fewer toward the northeast. Finally PC III, which contributes less to the relationship than the other PC's, has a coefficient indicating that ankle and foot elements are more frequent toward the southwest squares while head and neck elements are more frequent toward the northeast.

There are several similarities between the canonical correlation using the minimum and maximum element frequencies which should be mentioned. First in both analyses, there is only one axis which approaches or reaches significance at the 0.05 level. In both correlations that axis is in a northeast-southwest direction. In neither correlation does the other axis, the

Table 11. Canonical correlation coefficients of principal component scores for percentage of the Crow Creek Bed B maximum element count by excavation square.

Variables	V1	V2
Standardized Canonical Coefficients for the PC Variables		
PC I	-0.61000	-0.50882
PC II	0.69518	0.02425
PC III	-0.38028	0.86053
Standardized Canonical Coefficients for the Spatial Variables		
East-west	0.55793	-0.82989
North-south	0.82989	0.55793

northwest-southeast axis, reach significance. In both correlations skulls are found more frequently toward the northeast squares. Besides the similarities between the two correlations, there are differences, but because the two data sets lack comparability, nothing conclusive can be established.

The last part of this section deals with the articulated units. When the number of articulations from the two bone beds are compared, Bed B has proportionately more articulations than Bed A. Among the 17,380 bones and bone fragments, there are 1784 articulation numbers given in Bed B, while among the 175 elements in Bed A, there were only seven articulations. If the number of articulations is divided by the maximum element count, then Bed B's ratio is 0.1026 compared to Bed A's 0.040. The smaller proportion of articulations in Bed A suggests that the bones in that bed were more dismembered, more exposed, or exposed for a longer period than those in Bed B.

Inspecting the distribution of elementary articular groups from Bed B (Table 1) indicates that generally the larger elements and those located along the midsagittal plane are more frequently articulated than the smaller elements and those located more peripherally. The most frequently articulated elementary articular groups are those along the midline, beginning with the head and continuing through the lower back-sacrum. Next most frequently articulated are the lower arm and lower leg, pelvis, lower arm and arm. The articulations suggest that the body parts with more surrounding tissue are those most likely to remain articulated, especially those with substantial ligamentous, tendonous, and muscular tissue. It is an interesting exception that the lower arm and lower leg are more frequently articulated than the whole arm or whole leg.

The amount of disarticulation suggests that the bodies were exposed above ground for a considerable time or else much dismemberment occurred before the bodies were interred. It is difficult to estimate the time between death and burial. Because no insect remains were recovered, it seems likely that the bodies were exposed only during cold weather. Adult flies are generally absent in South Dakota between mid-October and late March (Gilbert and Bass 1967). Although it is possible that the bodies were exposed above ground during the Fall and through scavenging and movement of the bodies the maggots and pupal cases lost, this possibility seems unlikely. Insect remains undoubtedly would have been trapped in cavities and crevasses of the human bodies and included with the bodies when they were buried. It also seems unlikely that the pupal cases were overlooked during excavation. If the bodies were exposed only during cold weather, then they could have been exposed no longer than the five cold months when flies are absent. If the bodies were exposed in spring, decomposition and dismemberment may have progressed to the point that flies were not attracted to the bodies, although some other insects which are attracted to more decayed carcasses should have been present (cf. Ubelaker and Willey 1978). It seems likely that the deaths, exposure and burial all occurred within the five months of cold weather and probably happened in fewer than five months, perhaps in a month or even less.

Dismemberment probably explains more of the disarticulation than natural decomposition or time of exposure. While some of the dismemberment was apparently done by the raiders, where are so few cuts on the limbs that these explain only a small proportion of the dismemberments, and natural decomposition would have been slow during the cold months. Most of the dismemberments can be attributed to the scavengers based on the chew marks present on the bones. Dismemberment by raiders and by scavengers are discussed further in Chapter 6 which deals with mutilation.

C. Summary

There are at least 486 individuals represented by the elements from the excavations of the Crow Creek fortification ditch. The elements present are not all equally represented with the most frequently recovered ones tending to be the larger, denser bones located closer to the torso; the smaller, lighter more distal elements are less frequent. This absence may be explained by mutilation and dismemberment, destruction by scavengers, and omission by the people who recovered the buried bodies.

The stratigraphic, horizontal and articular context of the remains are examined. There are significant differences between some of the elements from the higher Bed A and deeper Bed B. Bed A contains proportionally more skull parts and fewer cervicals and thoracics than Bed B, while the proportions are reversed in Bed B. There are several possible explanations for these differences; a second gathering of the bones and subsequent burial, or scavenging and scattering of the buried remains by canids are the two most likely possibilities.

The horizontal distribution of the minimum and maximum element counts from Bed B are analyzed by canonical correlation. While there are discrepancies between the results based on the two counts, there are a few similarities as well. In both counts, the northeast-southwest axis is important while the northwest-southeast is not. Also important, skulls and skull parts are more frequent toward the northeast than the southwest squares. The similarities between the two counts suggest that placement in the ditch rather than physical influences, such as rolling down slope and natural sorting, may explain the significant element distributions.

The articular units are analyzed. Bed B contains a greater proportion of articulation than Bed A. Considering the articulations themselves, the larger elements and those along the midsagittal plane--especially those with substantial soft tissue attachments--are more frequently articulated. Nevertheless, the amount of disarticulation is impressive. The disarticulation suggests that the bodies were exposed above the ground for a considerable period and/or subject to much active dismemberment. It is likely, based on the absence of necrophagous insect remains, that the bodies were exposed sometime during the five cold months of the year, and based on modern decay rates, they may have been exposed less than a month.

Chapter 4
Crow Creek Paleodemography

Paleodemography has become a standard part of osteological analyses during the last several decades. Given its promise of gaining insights concerning mortality, morbidity, environment, and ecology, the inclusion of paleodemography is understandable.

All but a few paleodemographic osteological studies (e.g. Flinn et al. 1976, Turner and Morris 1970) have used samples from cemeteries, and apparently all studies have considered the samples mortality data. While it can be argued that the Crow Creek victims reflect mortality from a single cause and should be considered mortality data, Crow Creek is different from most osteological samples. This view does not, however, deny the utility of using the Crow Creek sample as mortality data if the paleodemography of the region or level of socio-cultural integration were being studied, but the unusual aspects of the Crow Creek sample need to be stressed.

Crow Creek presents a unique paleodemographic opportunity. Some of the unusual aspects of the sample are its large size, relatively early date, and southerly location in the Middle Missouri Region. From a paleodemographic perspective, what makes the Crow Creek sample unique are all of the unusual aspects listed above plus the extremely important circumstances of the victims.

The Crow Creek victims all died at a single point in time and from a single cause. The immediate cause of their death--warfare--froze the population structure of the Crow Creek villagers. And because of this freezing, the Crow Creek paleodemography is in some ways more comparable to a census of a modern-day, primitive village than the slowly accumulating mortality sample found buried in most cemeteries.

The purposes of this chapter are to describe the Crow Creek paleodemography and compare the Crow Creek age distribution with those of other skeletal samples from the same region. Based on the description and comparisons, the nature of the Crow Creek sample as mortality and census data is examined. A final purpose of this chapter is to estimate the number of people living in the Crow Creek Village so that number can be contrasted with the number of the individuals recovered by excavation.

A. Methods and Materials

There are two critical assessments, age and sex, which must be made from the skeletons to study paleodemography. The methods used to estimate age and sex are detailed here so they can be compared with those used on other samples (cf. Owsley 1975).

Age is estimated using two techniques: dental development for subadults and pubic symphysis morphology for adults. Subadult age is estimated using dental development because it is acknowledged as a more accurate estimator of chronological age than dental eruption or skeletal development. Because the dental standards of Moorrees et al. (1963a, 1963b) are considered the most accurate available (Merchant and Ubelaker 1977), they are employed here.

Both the maxillae and mandibles of subadults and those adults with open third molar roots were X-rayed so that dental development could be assessed. When both sides of the mandible or maxilla were present, the side with the more complete dental set was X-rayed. If both sides had equal dental sets, left maxillae and right mandibles were selected. To avoid duplication of fragmented jaws, only those pieces containing the second deciduous molar or second adult premolar tooth or crypt were included in the analysis.

All dental X-rays were taken and developed in the Department of Dental Hygiene at the University of South Dakota. Standard DF-58 film was used, employing a paralleling, long cone technique. Shooting and developing were done by Max Schmeling, Mark Swegle, and Jeff Swenson. Swegle scored the dental development using the X-rays and inspected the actual tooth when it could be removed from the alveolus.

Although the Moorrees et al. (1963a, 1963b) standards are almost entirely for mandibular teeth, maxillary teeth were also X-rayed, and age estimations for these were based on the mandibular standards. This approach was taken because there were far more maxillae than mandibles, and there appears to be little difference between dental development of the mandible and maxilla (Owsley 1978). To test for dental development differences between the mandible and maxilla, 50 mandible-maxilla pairs were aged independently and tested for statistical significance. A paired t-test was executed and found not significant ($\bar{d} = 0.19$, $T = 1.13$, $DF = 49$, $0.2 < P < 0.5$). Because of their similarities, the mandible and maxilla are used interchangeably. The subadult age distribution used here employs the maximum number of either maxilla or mandible, whichever was greater, for each age interval.

Nevertheless, there are problems in aging the maxillae which should be noted. Because the X-ray films were placed at an angle rather than parallel to the maxillary teeth more distortion is present than in the mandibular X-rays. It is also more difficult to consistently place the film packets on the maxilla than the mandible.

Adult ages were estimated using pubic symphysis morphology following the technique for young adult males by McKern and Stewart (1957), the technique for adult females by Gilbert and McKern (1973), and the phases for the oldest adult males by Todd (1921). When using the techniques of McKern and Stewart or Gilbert and McKern, their written description of the pubic changes and the plastic pubic symphysis casts were employed. Using the Todd method, the written description and an illustration of the male standards were used. Mark Swegle made all assessments.

There has been criticism of the Gilbert and McKern standards by Suchey (1979). Swegle found the standards by Gilbert and McKern more difficult to use than those of McKern and Stewart, and although not statistically tested, intraobserver error seemed to be substantial. Nevertheless, age estimation based on the Gilbert and McKern technique are retained in this analysis to make them comparable to the techniques used on the Larson Site skeletons.

Both the Gilbert and McKern, and McKern and Stewart techniques have a disadvantage when applied to the Crow Creek material. Both techniques present a mean and a range for each score, and the means sometimes skip the 5-year age intervals employed here. Thus, if the means alone were used, no individuals would be included in some of the intervals. Emphasizing the symphyseal age means causes fewer difficulties when other bones of the same individual are associated so other age-related features can be of assistance in estimating age. However when skeletons are disarticulated and symphysis change is used as the sole means of age estimation, then modifications to the means must be made.

In applying symphysis age standards to the Crow Creek material, four modifications are made. First, symphysis morphologies intermediate to two of the standards are rated the lower score plus 0.5. Second, assigning a score to an age category is modified so all 5-year age intervals are included. Table 12 shows which symphyseal scores are assigned to each interval. Third, males scoring 14 or 15 in the McKern and Stewart technique are aged using the stages of Todd (1921). This switch in male aging techniques is necessary because the base sample of McKern and Stewart was relatively young while that of Todd was old. Fourth, males scoring X in Todd's technique are arbitrarily divided in half, one-half placed in the 50-54 interval and the other half in the 55-59.

Besides age, the other important variable in a demographic profile is sex. Sex estimation was done only for adults, employed the pubis, and followed the criteria of Phenice (1969), which are regarded as a very reliable (Kelley 1978). Using the pubes for sex determination has the advantages of accuracy and usually the association of an ageable symphysis. The proportions of the sexes are compared to determine if either sex is disproportionately present. A binomial Z-test is calculated assuming a 1:1 sex ratio.

No attempt was made to determine subadult sex because of the difficulties in the assessment and the relative lack of accuracy. Nevertheless to consider the adult sexes separately, life table calculations require subadults to be sexed. This problem is overcome by dividing the number of unsexed subadults in each age interval in half. If the number of individuals is odd, the resulting 0.5 fraction is added to each sex. This artificial division is done for all age intervals 14 years and younger. These data are presented for the benefit of any future researcher who might wish to calculate vital statistics; none are calculated here.

Table 12. Pubic symphysis stages assigned to five-year intervals for estimating the adult Crow Creek ages.

Years	Females	Males
15-19	0 - 1[a]	0 - 2.5[b]
20-24	2 - 4	3 - 8.5
25-29	4.5 - 7	9 - 11.5
30-34	7.5 - 10	12 - 12.5
35-39	10.5 - 12	13
40-44	12.5	IX[c]
45-49	13	IX 1/2
50-54	13.5 - 14	X
55-59	14.5 - 15	X

[a]Female standards are from Gilbert and McKern (1973).

[b]Younger male standards are by McKern and Stewart (1957). Males scoring 14 or 15 in the McKern and Stewart standards are aged using the Todd system (1921).

[c]Older male standards are by Todd (1921).

A paleodemographic reconstruction requires that as many individuals as possible be included in the analysis. It is especially important to have an accurate estimation of subadult vs. adult numbers because such inaccuracies will distort the age distribution at death. These adjusted numbers, as calculated below, are used for comparisons of age and sex distributions of the Crow Creek sample itself.

The total number of accurately aged Crow Creek individuals is 337, a number considerably less than the minimum count of 486. Under-representation of ageable individuals is understandable given differential bone preservation and the osteological locations selected for estimating age. We would expect the more fragile pubic region, used to age and sex adults, to be more prone to damage and loss than the more durable teeth and jaws which were used to age the subadults.

To adjust any possible distortions and make as complete a paleodemographic sample as possible, the number of the most frequent element which could be aged as subadult or adult is used. The petrous portion of the temporal is ageable as adult or subadult and is the most frequent element at Crow Creek. There are 197 subadult right petrous portions (187 lefts) and 278 adult left petrous portions (237 rights). Comparing these numbers with the number of more accurately aged individuals, there are at least 45 subadults and 98 adults not represented in the more precisely aged sample. These extra 143 individuals are added to the 337 more precisely aged individuals to produce a more accurate paleodemographic picture. The ages of the remaining 6 individuals are still in doubt and are omitted from this analysis.

The 143 extra individuals are added to the more precisely aged individuals in the same proportions as the more accurately aged ones occur. Thus, the extra 45 less precisely aged subadults are added to the count in each of the age intervals from 0-1 through 10-14 based on the proportions of the more accurately aged individuals in each age interval. As an example, the 0-1 age interval contains 6.41 percent of the subadults. The 6.41 percent of 45 is 2.88 which is added to the number in that age interval. Adult numbers are similarly corrected, although the different proportions of the sexes require sex to be considered also. For example, the 20-24 year female interval contains 3.87 percent of all adults; 3.87 percent of the 98 unaged, unsexed adults amounts to 3.79, the number added to the original seven 20-24 year old females. After distributing the grossly aged 143 extra individuals, another manipulation is made.

It is necessary to smooth the age distributions because age estimation techniques, especially for the older adult ages, are relatively inaccurate and tend to artificially lump individuals in some intervals and exclude them from others. Smoothing also lessens any effect random variation may have on the age distribution of the sample when compared with the age distribution of the entire Crow Creek Village population. While it is impossible to know with certainty, the smoothed age distribution probably more accurately reflects the original Crow Creek population structure than the unsmoothed. The smoothed data are used primarily to compare Crow Creek with other comparably smoothed comparative samples.

Smoothing is executed using the three-mean moving average technique (Weiss 1973:15). Smoothing consists of adding the number of individuals in an age interval to those in the two adjacent categories, then dividing the sum by three. These calculations produce the smoothed number of individuals for the middle category. The process is repeated using the original and average numbers. There are a number of exceptions to this procedure which should be noted. Because of the unequal age intervals for the 0-1 and 1-4 categories contrasted with the other 5-year intervals, these shorter categories are not smoothed. The 5-9 year interval is smoothed in the normal way with the exception that 0.2 of the number from the 1-4 year interval is added to that interval to compensate for the shorter interval. The final interval (55-59) is not smoothed.

The Crow Creek population structure is described in three separate steps. First, the age distribution for the sexes combined is examined. Then, the sex ratio for the combined adult ages is examined. Finally, the distributions for the sexes separated are examined.

The Crow Creek sexes are combined to be compared with four skeletal samples. The four skeletal samples consist of two each from the Larson and Mobridge sites. These samples are the only large, comparably aged and sexed samples from the Middle Missouri Region. Both sites are located near Mobridge, South Dakota, in the north-central part of the state. The Larson Cemetery sample dates from 1750 to 1780 AD (Owsley and Bass 1979), and the Larson Village sample was apparently massacred about 1780 (Owsley and Bass 1979). However, it should be noted that there is recent evidence that Larson may date considerably earlier than the dates given here (O'Shea 1984). The Larson Cemetery paleodemographic data are from Owsley and Bass (1979:149, table 2) and the Larson Village data from Owsley et al. (1977:126, table 3). The Mobridge samples consist of two cemeteries. One cemetery is located west of the Mobridge Village (Mobridge 1) and is prehistoric, dating from 1600 to 1650 AD (Jantz 1973). The second Mobridge Site cemetery (Mobridge 2) is located south of the village and is protohistoric and possibly dates between 1700 and 1750 AD. The Mobridge mortality data are from Palkovich (1978:148, table 6; 149, table 7). The Mobridge data have already been smoothed by Palkovich but not the Larson data. Before using the Larson data, they are smoothed using the same technique described above.

To test for statistical differences among the samples, comparisons are made pair-wise between Crow Creek and the comparative samples. The two-tailed Kolmogorov-Smirnov two-sample test (Thomas 1976) is used which requires converting the age distribution to a cumulative percentage distribution. The comparisons which differ significantly using the Kolmogorov-Smirnov test are further examined using a X^2 test applied to the non-cumulative distribution of number of individuals. This additional step permits each age interval pair to be directly contrasted.

B. Results and Discussion

The Crow Creek age distribution counts for the combined sexes are described first (Table 13). In all three age distributions--unadjusted and unsmoothed, adjusted but unsmoothed, and adjusted and smoothed--there are deviations from the expected consistent decrease in numbers as age increases. For the combined sexes, the unadjusted and unsmoothed distribution count increases in the 5-9, 15-19, 30-34, 35-39, 45-49, and 55-59 intervals from the immediately preceding intervals. The adjusted but unsmoothed distribution count increases in the 5-9, 15-19, 30-34, 35-39, 45-49, and 55-59 intervals from

Table 13. Adjusting and smoothing the Crow Creek age distribution counts.

Age Interval	Unadjusted and Unsmoothed			Adjusted but Unsmoothed			Adjusted and Smoothed		
	Male	Female	Total	Male	Female	Total	Male	Female	Total
0 - 1	0	0	10	6.44	6.44	12.88	6.44	6.44	12.9
1 - 4	0	0	38	24.47	24.47	48.94	24.47	24.47	48.9
5 - 9	0	0	79	48.93	48.93	97.86	32.32	32.16	64.3
10 - 14	0	0	29	18.67	18.67	37.34	34.82	28.51	63.5
15 - 19	24	12	36	36.86	18.43	55.29	28.24	15.78	44.2
20 - 24	19	7	26	29.18	10.75	39.93	27.65	11.77	39.4
25 - 29	11	4	15	16.90	6.14	23.04	20.45	8.70	29.2
30 - 34	10	6	16	15.36	9.22	24.58	16.39	10.75	27.1
35 - 39	11	11	22	16.90	16.90	33.80	12.80	10.24	23.0
40 - 44	4	3	7	6.14	4.61	10.75	10.75	13.84	24.6
45 - 49	6	13	19	9.22	19.97	29.19	8.70	14.35	23.0
50 - 54	7	12	19	10.75	18.43	29.18	10.24	19.98	30.2
55 - 59	7	14	21	10.75	21.50	32.25	10.75	21.50	32.3

the immediately preceding ones. It is also unlikely that a normal population would have more females in the 55-59 interval than the 15-19 (Jaffe 1982). All of these instances differ from the expected distributions if Crow Creek were a bona fide census sample because a normal census would consistently decrease in numbers as age increases (Jaffe 1982). Based on the age distribution, Crow Creek cannot be considered census data.

The next paleodemographic result considered is the Crow Creek sex ratio for all adult ages combined. Of the 181 adults sexed by pubic morphology, 99 (54.7 percent) are male and 82 (45.3 percent) are female. To test whether there is a disproportionment number of one sex, a binomial Z-test is calculated assuming a 1:1 sex ratio. The result is not significant ($Z = 1.264$, $F(Z) = 0.896$, $P < 0.10$). Although there is some indication that more males than females are present, there is no statistical evidence that the sex ratio deviates from a 1:1 ratio when adult ages are combined.

However, if the sexes are divided by age interval, then significant differences are observed. In the adjusted and smoothed age distribution (Table 13), males out-number females by or almost by 2:1 in the 15-19, 20-24, 25-29, and 30-34 intervals. On the other hand, females out-number males by or almost by 2:1 in the 45-49, 50-54, and 55-59 intervals. These observations are supported by a X^2 test (Table 14) which shows that generally the males out-number the females in the younger intervals, while females out-number males in the older intervals ($X^2 = 20.68$, $DF = 3$, $P < 0.001$). It has been shown, then, that although there is no difference in the overall sex ratio, a significant difference does exist when age is considered.

Table 14. Comparison of the adjusted and smoothed Crow Creek adult age intervals by sex.

Age in Years	Males		Female	
	Expected	Observed	Expected	Observed
20-29	35.43	48.30	33.43	20.56
30-39	25.91	29.29	24.45	21.07
40-49	24.59	19.53	23.20	28.26
50-59	32.26	21.07	30.43	41.62

$X^2 = 20.68$, DF = 3, P < 0.001

These differences in the proportion of each sex based on age probably do not represent the actual sex ratios of the Crow Creek Village at the time of the attack, but likely show influences of the events which happened during and following the raid. Rarely if ever does a population have such disproportionate numbers of each sex by age (Jaffe 1982). The differences appear to be due to events which happened during or following the raid, and these deviations from a normal population further rule out the possibility that the Crow Creek sample is a census.

The relative lack of young females may have been caused by them being taken captive by the raiders, escaping from the village and massacre, or being killed but not recovered. Historic accounts occasionally mention Indian battles in which raiders attacked a group of men, women, and children. If the attack occurred in an exposed area or the defending group was out-numbered, the men generally tried to delay the attackers providing the women and children a chance to escape (e.g., Henry in Coues 1897:263). There is also historic mention of raiders killing men, but taking at least some women and children captive (Tabeau 1939:150) and presumably taking them to the camp of the raiders. The third explanation for the absence of the younger females--them being killed but not recovered--remains a possibility, although it is difficult to judge how likely it is.

The relative absence of older males might be explained by them escaping from the village and massacre or being killed but for some reason not recovered in our excavations. It is also possible that the absence of older males is a demographic reality, the males having been subjected to higher mortality than the females throughout the period preceding the massacre. It is difficult to judge the relative likelihood of these possibilities.

Having described and discussed the Crow Creek paleodemography, Crow Creek is now compared with another massacre sample and other cemetery samples from the same region using the percentage of individuals in each age interval (Table 15). When Crow Creek is compared with the photohistoric Larson Village massacre sample (Table 16), no significant differences are observed in the age distributions. This result suggests that massacre age distributions are similar in both prehistoric and protohistoric times.

On the other hand, when Crow Creek is compared with the age distribution at the Mobridge and Larson cemeteries (Table 17), highly significant differences are observed. Chi-square tests (Tables 18, 19, 20) are calculated to determine which cells contribute most to the significance noted. In all three X^2's, the Crow Creek sample is under-represented in the 0-9 interval and over-represented in nearly all other age intervals. The only exception to the Crow Creek over-representation in age intervals after 0-9 is the 40-49 interval of Mobridge 2, and these expected and observed values are approximately equal. These results suggest that the Crow Creek age distribution is dissimilar from mortality data and cannot be considered a normal mortality sample.

Because of the similarities between the Crow Creek and Larson Village massacre samples, they are combined and compared with the combined cemetery samples used in the previous comparisons. The results are similar to those when Crow Creek alone was compared with the cemeteries. There are highly significant differences between the massacre and cemetery samples (Table 21). When individual cells are examined (Table 22), the massacre samples are under-represented in the 0-9 interval and over-represented in the subsequent intervals, as expected based on the comparisons with Crow Creek alone.

Table 15. Adjusted and smoothed age distribution frequencies at Crow Creek for each sex and total sample.

Age Interval	Male	Female	Total
0	2.62	2.92	2.76
1 - 4	9.95	11.09	10.49
5 - 9	13.41	14.93	14.13
10 - 14	14.44	13.30	13.90
15 - 19	11.52	7.24	9.49
20 - 24	11.28	5.35	8.48
25 - 29	8.36	3.96	6.28
30 - 34	6.68	4.89	5.83
35 - 39	5.23	4.66	4.96
40 - 44	4.39	6.28	5.28
45 - 49	3.55	6.52	4.96
50 - 54	4.18	9.08	6.50
55 - 59	4.39	9.78	6.94
	100.00	100.00	100.00

Table 16. Smoothed Crow Creek age distribution compared with the smoothed Larson Village sample. Maximum difference is underlined.

Age in Years	Crow Creek Cumulative Percent	Larson Village Cumulative Percent	Difference
0 - 9	27.38	23.44	3.94
10 - 19	50.77	47.39	3.38
20 - 29	65.53	71.87	-6.34
30 - 39	76.32	88.54	-12.22
40 - 49	86.56	99.99	<u>-13.43</u>
50 - 59	100.00	99.99	0.01
Sample size	467	64	
0.10 critical value			16.26
0.05 critical value			18.13
Conclusion			No difference

Table 17. Smoothed age distribution of Crow Creek compared with those of Middle Missouri Region cemetery samples. Maximum differences are underlined.

Age in Years	Crow Creek Cumulative Percentage	Mobridge 1 Cumulative Percentage	Mobridge 1 Difference	Mobridge 2 Cumulative Percentage	Mobridge 2 Difference	Larson Cemetery Cumulative Percentage	Larson Cemetery Difference
0 - 9	27.38	69.94	-42.56*	48.20	-20.82*	53.88	-26.50*
10 - 19	50.77	74.54	-23.77	59.71	- 8.94	76.01	-25.24
20 - 29	65.53	80.29	-14.76	70.81	- 5.28	83.54	-18.01
30 - 39	76.32	86.53	-10.21	80.18	- 3.86	90.57	-14.25
40 - 49	86.56	92.61	- 6.05	91.16	- 4.60	96.60	-10.04
50 - 59	100.00	100.00	0.00	100.00	0.00	100.00	0.00
Sample size	467	203		249		735	
0.001 critical value			16.39		15.30		11.54

* Significant at 0.001 level of confidence.

Table 18. Comparison of the smoothed age counts of Crow Creek and Mobridge 1.

Age in Years	Crow Creek		Mobridge 1	
	Expected	Observed	Expected	Observed
0 - 9	188.2	128	81.8	142
10 - 19	82.2	109	35.8	9
20 - 29	56.5	69	24.5	12
30 - 39	43.9	50	19.1	13
40 - 49	41.8	48	18.2	12
50 - 59	54.4	63	23.6	15

$X^2 = 111.82$, DF = 5, P < 0.001

Table 19. Comparison of the smoothed age counts of Crow Creek and Mobridge 2.

Age in Years	Crow Creek		Mobridge 2	
	Expected	Observed	Expected	Observed
0 - 9	161.8	128	86.2	120
10 - 19	90.0	109	48.0	29
20 - 29	63.3	69	33.7	28
30 - 39	47.6	50	25.4	23
40 - 49	48.9	48	26.1	27
50 - 59	55.4	63	29.6	22

$X^2 = 36.71$, DF = 5, $P < 0.001$

Table 20. Comparison of smoothed age counts of Crow Creek and Larson Cemetery.

Age in Years	Crow Creek		Larson Cemetery	
	Expected	Observed	Expected	Observed
0 - 9	203.6	128	320.4	396
10 - 19	105.7	109	166.3	163
20 - 29	48.2	69	75.8	55
30 - 39	39.6	50	62.4	52
40 - 49	35.7	48	56.3	44
50 - 59	34.2	63	53.8	25

$X^2 = 111.82$, DF = 5, P < 0.001.

Table 21. Comparison of the smoothed cumulative percentages of the two combined massacre samples with that of the three combined cemetery samples. Maximum difference is underlined.

Age in Years	Massacres	Cemeteries	Difference
0 - 9	26.91	55.43	<u>-28.52</u>
10 - 19	50.37	72.36	-21.99
20 - 29	66.30	80.36	-14.06
30 - 39	77.80	87.77	- 9.97
40 - 49	88.19	94.76	- 6.57
50 - 59	100.00	99.98	0.02
Sample Size	531	1187	
0.001 critical value			10.18
Conclusion	Significant difference		

Table 22. Comparison of the smoothed age counts of the two combined massacre samples with that of the three combined cemetery samples.

Age in Years	Massacres		Cemeteries	
	Expected	Observed	Expected	Observed
0 - 9	247.6	143	553.4	658
10 - 19	100.5	124	224.5	201
20 - 29	55.6	85	124.4	95
30 - 39	46.1	61	102.9	88
40 - 49	42.7	55	95.3	83
50 - 59	38.6	63	86.2	62

$X^2 = 128.83$, DF = 5, P < 0.001

The next question to be answered is, what proportion of the total village population is included in the bone bed? To answer this question, an estimation of the number of people living in the Crow Creek Village is needed to contrast with the number recovered in the bone beds.

An estimation of the number of people living at Crow Creek is possible based on the number of lodges at the site and the number of people living in each lodge. To make the estimation, assumptions must be made that the average number of people living in each lodge was the same as it was during the historic period when the number of individuals and lodges were recorded, the lodges at Crow Creek were all inhabited at the same time, and all lodges at the site were counted.

Given these assumptions, the two critical numbers in estimating the Crow Creek population are the number of lodges at the site and the number of people per lodge. Kivett and Jensen (1976:68) in their report on the Crow Creek Site write that there are at least 50 lodges from the Initial Coalescent component. To estimate the number of individuals per lodge, Roberts (1977:1974, fig. 35) has provided formulae based on historic accounts. His figure for the number of people per lodge for Arikara is 16.62 and for lodges of any tribal affiliation is almost 15 (14.88). Multiplying these figures by the 50 lodges indicates that at least 744 (any tribal affiliation) or 831 (Arikara) lived at the site.

That these are minimum figures cannot be stressed enough. One reason these figures must be considered minimal is because the village appears to have been expanding, which suggests that all or nearly all of the lodges were inhabited. The 50 lodge count is considered a minimum count by Kivett and Jensen, and it is entirely possible that there are other, silted-over lodges in the lower, southwestern part of the village.

Having estimated a minimum number of people living at Crow Creek and having established a minimum number of skeletons represented, it is appropriate to compare the two. Using the larger estimation of village population (831) and the minimum number of skeletons (486), it seems that only about 60 percent of the village population is represented by the skeletons in the ditch.

There are a number of possible explanations why the other 345 individuals or 40 percent are missing. First of all, it is possible that the number of skeletons represented in the ditch or the estimation of the number of people living at Crow Creek are inaccurate. Secondly, we know that there is additional, unrecovered skeletal material continuing east from the rest of the deposit in the fortification ditch, so not all of the material was recovered. There may be additional remains present elsewhere in the ditch, the village, or outside the village. Material may also have been destroyed by natural causes and thus not recoverable. Additional possibilities are that some of the village members were absent when the raid occurred, some were able to escape from the village during the raid, or some were taken captive.

C. Summary

This chapter is divided into three parts: comparisons between sexes and among age intervals in the Crow Creek sample; comparisons between Crow Creek, another massacre sample, and the cemetery samples; and estimation of the proportions of the Crow Creek Village population represented by the skeletons.

The age structure of Crow Creek is irregular and there are deviations in the sex ratio by age. Some older age intervals contain more individuals than the immediately preceding, younger age intervals. These perturbations are observed in the overall age distribution as well as in both age distributions by sex. The sex ratio for all adults approaches a 1:1 ratio, but when the sexes are considered by age, differences are apparent. In general, the young males out-number the young females, while the old females out-number the old males. From these deviations in the age and age-by-sex structure, it is apparent that the skeletal sample from Crow Creek is typical of neither normal mortality nor normal census data. There are several possible explanations for these observations. The relative absence of young females may have been caused by them being taken captive by the raiders. Their absence as well as the absence of the old males may have been caused by them escaping from the village and massacre, or being killed but not recovered.

The Crow Creek age distribution for the sexes combined is compared with that of another massacre sample and three cemetery samples. There is no difference between Crow Creek and the other massacre sample, but there are marked differences between Crow Creek and the cemetery samples, principally in the youngest age intervals. When both massacres are combined and compared with the combined cemetery samples, the same trend is found: namely, there is a significant difference between the massacre and cemetery samples and the difference is greatest in the 0-9 year interval. There seems to be some over-all similarity between the population structure of massacre victims from the Middle Missouri Region which differs from that of cemeteries from the same region.

An estimation of the proportion of the Crow Creek Village population which was recovered in the excavations is made. Although based on many assumptions and subject to considerable error, it appears that about 60 percent of the village is represented by the excavated sample.

Chapter 5
Crow Creek Cranial Affinities

On the Northern Plains, cranial measurements and discrete traits have been used to estimate morphological affinities. There have been a variety of interesting results, including studies of microevolutionary changes (Bass 1964; Jantz 1970, 1972, 1973, 1977; Key 1983; Key and Jantz, 1981) and ethnic distinctions (Jantz 1974, 1976, 1977; Jantz et al. 1978; Key 1983; Ubelaker and Jantz, 1979). Nearly all of these studies employ cranial measurements.

The Crow Creek cranial sample is important because there are no other large Middle Missouri Region cranial samples as early or as far south as Crow Creek. Crow Creek is important because it links the earlier Central Plains Tradition with the later Arikara samples both geographically and temporally. In particular, Crow Creek may shed light on the origins of and the relationship between the Arikara and Pawnee. Using the Crow Creek morphological distances, three problems are studied. Two problems involve variation among the Crow Creek crania and the third compares the Crow Creek sample with the other samples.

There have been relatively few within-site analyses of Middle Missouri Region skeletal material (e.g., Owsley 1981, Owsley and Jantz 1978), and none have dealt solely with a single component within a site. Crow Creek offers an excellent opportunity to study within-site variation of a single component. Looking for variation within the Crow Creek sample, two analyses are performed. Principal component scores from cranial measurements are employed in an outlier analysis to determine whether morphologically dissimilar skulls are present in the sample. If there are morphologically dissimilar skulls present, it might indicate some raiders were buried with their victims or that mate-exchange was occurring between groups. The second within-site analysis employs the principal component scores to inspect the cranial variation by where the skulls were interred. Cranial variation and burial location are studied to see if placement in the fortification ditch is associated with morphology. If heterogeneity is present, it may indicate that the skulls and perhaps the postcranial skeletons were separated into groups for burial. Such heterogeneity among portions of the bone bed might indicate placement based on kin affiliations. Both studies employ cranial measurements only.

The third analysis compares Crow Creek cranial measurements and cranial discrete traits with other samples from the Northern and Central Plains. The purpose of this analysis is to determine Crow Creek's morphological similarities with other samples and to suggest temporal and tribal affiliations.

A. Methods and Materials

All relatively complete Crow Creek skulls were reconstructed by Mark Swegle and Willey during January 1979. Altogether measurements were taken on 104 skulls and 102 were observed. Willey took all measurements and observations.

For the purposes of these cranial analyses, only those skulls with 15 measurements which previously had been taken on other comparable samples are used. The measurements employed are glabella-occipital length (GOL), maximum cranial breadth (XCB), basion-bregma (BBH), basion-nasion (BNL), basion-prosthion (BPL), minimum frontal breadth (WFB), bizygomatic breadth (ZYB), nasion-alveolare (NPH), external alveolar length (EAL), external alveolar breadth (EAB), nasal height (NLH), nasal breadth (NLB), bifrontal chord (FMB), basion-biporion (BPO), and auricular height (AUH). These measurements have been fully described elsewhere (Bass 1964, 1971; Jantz 1970), and additional comments have already been published (Zimmerman et al. 1981: 125-129). All 15 measurements were taken on 30 female and 33 male skulls.

Four additional skulls were added to the analyzed sample. Of these, three were missing one measurement and one was missing two measurements. Skull 11, a female, was missing AUH; Skull 284, a male, was missing FMB; and Skull 368, a male, was missing ZYB. Skull 370, a female, was lacking ZYB and FMB. These missing measurements were estimated using multiple regression formulae which employed all of the other measurements present. The regressions were performed separately for each sex using the GLM routine in SAS (SAS Institute 1979). With these four skulls added to the Crow Creek sample, a total of 67 (32 female, 35 male) skulls were analyzed. Descriptive statistics were calculated for each sex using the CONDESCRIPTIVE program in SPSS (Nie et al. 1975) and are presented in Tables 23 and 24. Principal component analyses were performed for each sex using the SPSS program (Nie et al. 1975). The principal component scores are used in the outlier analysis and to check for cranial heterogeneity in burial location.

The outlier analysis is performed using the principal component scores of cranial measurements to determine if morphologically dissimilar skulls were present in the ditch. All 15 principal component scores of each individual are used to calculate D^2 from the group's centroid for the individual using a program written by William W. Baden. Those crania falling beyond the 0.05 limit are suspect.

Table 23. Descriptive statistics of female Crow Creek cranial measurements. Statistics are based on 32 female crania with full complement of measurements. All numbers are in millimeters.

Measurements	Mean	Standard Deviation	Minimum	Maximum	Range
GOL	170.22	4.72	160	181	21
XCB	142.31	5.69	129	151	22
BBH	132.53	4.04	125	142	17
BNL	100.50	4.24	91	112	21
BPL	97.38	5.05	86	109	23
WFB	91.56	4.04	83	98	15
ZYB	132.88	4.46	123	139	16
NPH	69.94	3.45	63	77	14
EAL	51.59	2.94	46	57	11
EAB	64.22	3.84	56	71	15
NLH	50.19	2.22	45	54	9
NLB	26.38	1.93	22	31	9
FMB	98.94	3.34	93	105	12
BPO	19.56	3.53	12	28	16
AUH	116.94	4.19	109	130	21

Table 24. Descriptive statistics of male Crow Creek cranial measurements. Statistics are based on 35 male crania with full complement of measurements. All numbers are in millimeters.

Measurements	Mean	Standard Deviation	Minimum	Maximum	Range
GOL	176.09	6.86	163	190	27
XCB	145.43	6.42	131	162	31
BBH	136.11	4.96	124	145	21
BNL	104.63	4.71	95	116	21
BPL	102.66	4.72	93	112	19
WFB	95.29	4.78	87	105	18
ZYB	140.49	7.12	126	155	29
NPH	73.80	3.72	67	81	14
EAL	54.06	3.10	49	60	11
EAB	67.97	3.04	62	79	17
NLH	53.80	3.11	47	59	12
NLB	27.46	1.80	23	31	8
FMB	103.54	4.00	94	111	17
BPO	20.17	3.29	11	25	14
AUH	120.57	4.25	111	128	17

The measurable skulls are also tested for morphological heterogeneity based on the location they were found and the principal component scores. The skulls are separated by excavation units. Because the sample size for each individual square is so small, skulls from all squares with the same number are combined. Thus, for example, the crania from squares 5A, 5B and 5C are lumped together for the analysis. This lumping allows testing of differences among groups of skulls on the east-west orientation but not the north-south. This compromise is necessary because the sample of each individual square is too small for statistical analysis. This compromise is also justified because the north-south placement of the crania is probably largely due to how steep the slope of bones was, and there is better access to the ditch in the east-west direction than the north-south. It seems likely, then, that if cultural distinctions were being made, they would be in an east-west orientation. Another compromise is made. Because of the very small number of skulls from combined Squares 9 and combined Squares 10, these two are also combined (Table 25).

The male and female skulls are divided by combined squares and analyzed with the discriminate subprogram in SPSS (Nie et al. 1975). The principal component scores for each individual are employed. In addition to these analyses of variation within the Crow Creek sample, skulls are used to estimate morphological distances between Crow Creek and those from other sites.

Two approaches to establish cranial morphological distances between Crow Creek and other samples from the Central and Northern Plains are used. In the past, cranial measurements have been frequently used to study morphological relationships of Northern Plains samples. The other approach, discrete traits, has been used less frequently. Here

Table 25. Samples from Crow Creek squares combined for analyzing cranial morphology homogeneity among the squares.

Squares	Females	Males
5 A,B,C	11	7
6 A,B,C	4	8
7 A,B,C	6	6
8 A,B,C	7	7
9 and 10 A,B,C	4	7

cranial measurements are employed to estimate morphological distances and to classify individual crania into groups. The cranial discrete traits are used only to estimate morphological distances.

The cranial measurement morphological distances between Crow Creek and 11 other samples from the Northern and Central Plains are estimated using the canonical variates calculated from the raw measurements and the discriminant subprogram of SPSS (Nie et al. 1975). All crania from the other 11 samples were measured by R.L. Jantz, using the same measurement techniques as those used on the Crow Creek material. Information concerning those samples is presented in Jantz (1972, 1974). For the most part, each sample consists of skulls from single sites, although sample sizes for Mandan, Omaha, Pawnee and Ponca are so small that skulls from several sites are combined.

Another way to examine intersite and intergroup differences using craniometrics is classifying individuals into the group with the closest group centroid. Thus, rather than simply examining the placement of group centroids relative to one another, individual variability is considered by seeing into which groups individuals are misclassified. This statistical manipulation is performed by using an option in the same SPSS program (Nie et al. 1975) which is used to produce the canonical variate values. A hit-miss table results when the individual results are combined. A _hit_ is an individual correctly identified to its group and a _miss_ is incorrectly identified.

In addition to the distances calculated based on craniometric data, discrete traits are used. As many as 20 paired and nine single cranial and mandibular discrete traits were observed on each of the 102 skulls and 49 associated mandibles. For the purpose of this analysis, only 16 of the 29 observations are employed. These 16 traits were selected because Jantz (1970:70, table 12) found no sex differences in trait frequency in a larger, similar sample, thus allowing the sexes to be combined. The 16 observations used are lambdoidal ossicle (medial and lateral), parietal foramen, coronal ossicle, epipteric bone, ossicle in a the mastoid suture, anterior condylar canal double, accessory palatine foramen, supraorbital foramen complete, frontal foramen, accessory infraorbital foramen, accessory mental foramen, ossicle at lambda, inca bone, pharyngeal fossa and superior sagittal sinus turns left. All of these observations are recommended by Berry and Berry (1967), except ossicle in the mastoid suture which Jantz noted. Paired observations are combined to get frequencies. Before mentioning the comparative samples and the statistic used, some definitions of terms and method descriptions are necessary.

Ossicles are isolated pieces of bone in sutures which are large enough (usually greater than or equal to 1cm in diameter) to be observed without difficulty. Exceptions to this rule are epipteric bones, where even the smallest ossicle is noted as being present. Sometimes it is difficult to judge whether or not an ossicle near the juncture of two sutures is at that point or on one of the other sutures. The major example are bones in the lambdoidal area. Bones near the junctures are called ossicles at those joints if, and only if, the ossicle had a side formed by each of the sutures.

Extra foramina generally have to be larger than a pin-point to be counted. Any foramen near the palatine foramen is recorded as accessory. Recording the supraorbital foramen/notch was somewhat eclectic, and earlier in taking the observations some frontal foramina may have been mistakenly identified as supraorbital foramina. Accessory infraorbital foramina are especially difficult to identify. In some skulls, there seems to be a zone ringing the infraorbital region, especially laterally and medially to the orbit, where the accessory foramina are common. Accessory foramina are identified as accessory infraorbital foramina only if they are present within the distance of the diameter of the infraorbital foramen measured from the nearest edge of the infraorbital foramen. Thus, supernumerary foramina occurring on the frontal process of the maxilla are excluded.

It is frequently hard to judge whether or not a pharyngeal fossa is present. In borderline cases, if the depression is large enough to both see and feel, a pharyngeal fossa is noted as present.

Usually the turning of the superior sagittal sinus is obvious, but in some cases it is not apparent. In these cases, the sizes of the transverse sulcii are inspected with the larger sulcus presumed to indicate the direction the sagittal sinus was turned.

In brief, these "discrete" nonmetric observations are often indistinct. There seems to be room for observer interpretation, but it is hoped that these definitions and the description of methods are reproducible.

All of the comparative discrete trait samples, except one, are from Jantz (1970). The sample not previously published is the St. Helena (25CD4, 25CD7, 25DK9, 25DK10 and 25DK13) which was kindly made available by Jantz. The Crow Creek sample used is comprised of the same crania used in metric analysis, except for one male (Skull 294) for which no observations were recorded. A relatively simple statistical procedure is used. Following Grewal (1962) and Berry and Berry (1967), the frequencies of the 16 traits are converted to an angle, expressed in radians (θ), and the distance between samples calculated based on the difference between radians.

B. Results and Discussion

The outlier analysis was performed to see if morphologically dissimilar skulls were present in the ditch. The presence of different kinds of skulls might mean that some raiders were buried with their victims or mate-exchange occurred. There are, of course, other possible explanations. All 15 components from each individual were employed to calculate Mahalanobis' D^2 from the group's centroid for individual crania. Not one of the 32 female (Table 26) or 35 male (Table 27) crania fell in the 0.05 probability range. Therefore, the null hypothesis--that there are no significantly different skulls present--must be accepted. The measurable skulls all appear to belong to a homogenous group, the Crow Creek Village inhabitants.

The skulls were tested also for morphological heterogeneity by location in the ditch. Heterogeneity among the excavation squares might indicate kin-aligned burial. The females have four components greater than 1.0. The males have five components with eigenvalues greater than 1.0, but the sixth has an eigenvalue (0.99787) so close to 1.0 that it is included here. Thus the males are analyzed using six components. No statistically significant differences are present in either sex. Cranial measurements do not vary with east-west position in the ditch.

Table 26. D^2 values of individual Crow Creek female crania from the group centroid. None is statistically significant. DF = 15

Skull Number	D^2 Value	Probability
11	12.04	0.50 - 0.25
21	20.86	0.25 - 0.10
22	18.69	0.25 - 0.10
35	20.78	0.25 - 0.10
57	15.08	0.50 - 0.25
61	13.09	0.75 - 0.50
66	13.60	0.75 - 0.50
76	23.26	0.10 - 0.05
94	10.98	0.90 - 0.75
96	9.67	0.90 - 0.75
98	14.45	0.50 - 0.25
103	10.39	0.90 - 0.75
145	18.79	0.25 - 0.10
156	16.89	0.50 - 0.25
173	18.82	0.25 - 0.10
190	16.48	0.25 - 0.10
195	11.67	0.75 - 0.50
196	11.02	0.90 - 0.75
197	10.93	0.90 - 0.75
207	6.95	0.975- 0.95
228	12.46	0.75 - 0.50
233	16.66	0.50 - 0.25
308	21.17	0.25 - 0.10
315	18.06	0.50 - 0.25
322	9.22	0.90 - 0.75
323	14.65	0.50 - 0.25
331	12.38	0.75 - 0.50
336	9.18	0.90 - 0.75
361	8.03	0.95 - 0.90
363	14.43	0.50 - 0.25
370	15.62	0.50 - 0.25
377	14.10	0.75 - 0.50

Table 27. D^2 values of individual Crow Creek male crania from the group centroid. None is statistically significant. DF = 15

Skull Number	D^2 Value	Probability
1	12.04	0.75 - 0.50
8	10.22	0.90 - 0.75
12	17.31	0.50 - 0.25
18	20.47	0.25 - 0.10
51	12.27	0.75 - 0.50
63	12.59	0.75 - 0.50
83	15.19	0.50 - 0.25
91	15.14	0.50 - 0.25
95	21.79	0.25 - 0.10
100	11.52	0.75 - 0.50
108	15.78	0.50 - 0.25
134	13.40	0.75 - 0.50
135	13.95	0.75 - 0.50
151	13.02	0.75 - 0.50
186	11.43	0.75 - 0.50
216	11.76	0.75 - 0.50
218	11.10	0.75 - 0.50
229	13.15	0.75 - 0.50
236	13.99	0.75 - 0.50
265	21.13	0.25 - 0.10
269	13.90	0.75 - 0.50
284	22.17	0.25 - 0.10
286	15.37	0.50 - 0.25
294	16.24	0.50 - 0.25
301	12.13	0.75 - 0.50
302	10.84	0.90 - 0.75
306	21.15	0.25 - 0.10
307	18.71	0.25 - 0.10
317	16.35	0.50 - 0.25
348	9.32	0.90 - 0.75
356	5.68	0.99 - 0.975
358	8.81	0.90 - 0.75
360	21.89	0.25 - 0.10
368	16.20	0.50 - 0.25
392	14.00	0.75 - 0.50

Two approaches to estimate cranial morphological distances between Crow Creek and other cranial samples are employed: namely, cranial measurements and cranial discrete traits. The craniometric results are discussed first.

In the craniometric analysis, the first four canonical variates are statistically significant in both sexes. The results in both sexes are so similar that they can be discussed together. The first canonical variate (CV I), which explains 35.7 percent of the female variability and 43.1 percent of the male, primarily separates Crow Creek and to a lesser extent the St. Helena sites (25DK9 and 25DK13) from the Mandan (Fig. 3). It may be that some of the differences are due to interobserver error (cf. Utermohle and Zegura 1982), although both observers were trained by the same instructor so differences should be minimal. CV I arranges the Arikara sites from northern South Dakota (Mobridge, Rygh, Larson and Leavenworth) chronologically, and it appears to be doing the same with Crow Creek and possibly the St. Helena sites.

The second canonical variate (CV II) explains 33.3 percent and 24.3 percent of the female and male variability, respectively (Fig. 3). CV II mainly separates the Omaha, Ponca, and to a lesser extent the Pawnee from the other samples, especially the Arikara groups. Generally CV II seems to be geographically influenced, with the southern groups at one end and the northern groups at the other. The Mandan are a notable exception to this generalization. Crow Creek falls near the center of the distribution, near the St. Helena (25DK9 and 25DK13) and near some Arikara samples.

The third canonical variate (CV III), which explains 13.2 percent and 10.7 percent of the female and male variability, respectively, separates the Mandan and St. Helena (25DK9

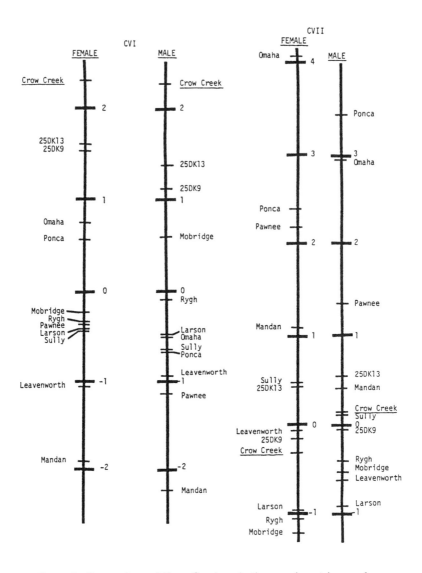

Figure 3. Comparison of Crow Creek and other craniometric samples on canonical variates I and II.

and 25DK13) samples from the Omaha, Ponca, and at least some of the Arikara samples (Fig. 4). There is no clear patterning to the distribution. Crow Creek again falls near the center of the distribution, near the Pawnee and some of the Arikara samples.

The fourth and final canonical variate (CV IV), which explains 6.0 percent and 7.9 percent of the female and male variability, respectively, is difficult to interpret because the female and male plots are somewhat different (Fig. 4). The female CV IV separates the Ponca, earlier Arikara (Mobridge, Rygh, and Sully), and 25DK9 from the Omaha and later Arikara (Larson and Leavenworth). The female Crow Creek sample falls among the Mandan, Pawnee, and 25DK13. The male CV IV, on the other hand, separates both St. Helena sites (25DK9 and 25DK13) and some earlier Arikara (Mobridge and Rygh) from the Omaha, Mandan, one of the later Arikara (Leavenworth), and Crow Creek.

Each CV is interesting in itself, but discussing them individually makes trends difficult to grasp. CV's can be combined in multi-dimensional plots, thus making patterns more apparent. Simultaneously plotting CV I, II, and III (Figs. 5 and 6) displays the maximum variability on 3 axes--82.2 percent of the female and 78.1 percent of the male variability. Both sexes of Crow Creek rest closest to the St. Helena sites (25DK9 and 25DK13); next closest are the earlier Arikara sites.

In addition to examining the group centroids, the hit-miss tables can be inspected to gain an appreciation of variation within the groups (Tables 28 and 29). Before considering the incorrect identifications, a few comments concerning the correct identifications are necessary.

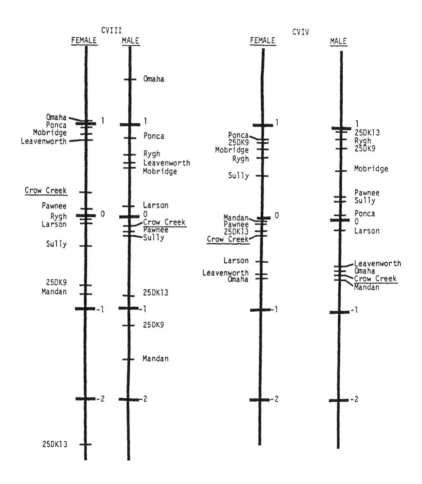

Figure 4. Comparison of Crow Creek and other craniometric samples on canonical variates III and IV.

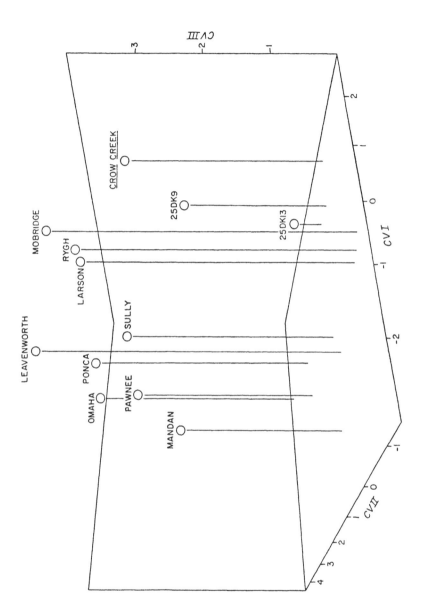

Figure 5. Crow Creek female and other female craniometric group centroids displayed on canonical variates I, II, and III.

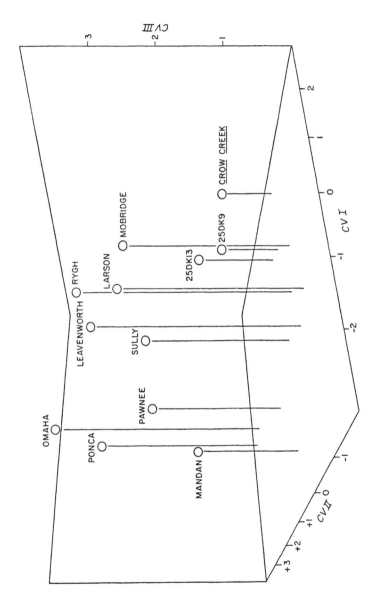

Figure 6. Crow Creek male and other male craniometric group centroids displayed on canonical variates I, II, and III.

Table 28. Hit-miss distribution of female Crow Creek and other female cranial samples. Numbers in parentheses are percentages.

	Crow Creek	Leaven-worth	Larson	Sully	Mobridge	Rygh	Ponca	Omaha	Mandan	Pawnee	25DK9	25DK13
Crow Creek	25 (78.1)	0	0	0	2 (6.3)	1 (3.1)	0	0	0	0	3 (9.4)	1 (3.1)
Leavenworth	0	12 (63.2)	2 (10.5)	0	2 (10.5)	1 (5.3)	0	0	1 (5.3)	1 (5.3)	0	0
Larson	0	4 (8.5)	27 (57.4)	2 (4.3)	3	8 (17.0)	0	0	0	2 (4.3)	0	0
Sully	1 (3.6)	3 (10.7)	2 (7.1)	8 (28.6)	1 (3.6)	2 (7.1)	1 (3.6)	0	6 (21.4)	2 (7.1)	2 (7.1)	1 (2.1)
Mobridge	1 (5.9)	1	1	0	11 (64.7)	3 (17.6)	0	0	0	0	0	0
Rygh	0	0	3 (17.6)	1 (5.9)	2 (11.8)	7 (41.2)	0	0	1 (5.9)	0	1 (5.9)	2 (11.8)
Ponca	0	0	0	0	0	0	5 (62.5)	1 (12.5)	1	0	1 (12.5)	0
Omaha	0	0	0	0	0	0	1 (14.3)	6 (85.7)	0	0	0	0
Mandan	0	1 (5.6)	1 (5.6)	1 (5.6)	0	0	0	0	15 (83.3)	0	0	0
Pawnee	0	0	0	1 (20.0)	0	0	0	0	0	4 (80.0)	0	0
25DK9	0	0	0	0	0	0	0	0	0	0	2 (50.0)	2 (50.0)
25DK13	0	0	0	0	0	0	0	0	0	0	2 (22.2)	7 (77.8)

Table 29. Hit-miss distribution of male Crow Creek and other male cranial samples. Numbers in parentheses are percentages.

	Crow Creek	Leavenworth	Larson	Sully	Mo-bridge	Rygh	Ponca	Omaha	Mandan	Pawnee	25DK9	25DK13
Crow Creek	23 (65.7)	0	0	2 (5.7)	2 (5.7)	3 (8.6)	0	0	0	1 (2.9)	2 (5.7)	2 (5.7)
Leavenworth	0	14 (70.0)	3 (15.0)	2 (10.0)	0	0	0	0	0	1 (5.0)	0	0
Larson	3 (6.7)	7 (15.6)	18 (40.0)	2 (4.4)	8 (17.8)	5 (11.1)	0	0	0	2 (4.4)	0	0
Sully	1 (2.7)	4 (10.8)	6 (16.2)	7 (18.9)	0	7 (18.9)	0	0	5 (13.5)	4 (10.8)	3 (8.1)	0
Mobridge	2 (11.8)	0	3 (17.6)	1 (5.9)	8 (47.1)	2 (11.8)	0	0	0	1 (5.9)	0	0
Rygh	1 (6.7)	1 (6.7)	0	1 (6.7)	2 (13.3)	8 (53.3)	0	0	0	0	0	2 (13.3)
Ponca	0	0	0	0	0	0	4 (67.7)	2 (33.3)	0	0	0	0
Omaha	0	0	0	0	0	0	0	4 (80.0)	0	1 (20.0)	0	0
Mandan	0	0	0	1 (8.3)	0	0	0	0	10 (83.3)	1 (8.3)	0	0
Pawnee	0	0	0	0	1 (11.1)	0	0	0	0	8 (88.9)	0	0
25DK9	1 (25.0)	0	0	0	0	0	0	0	0	0	2 (50.0)	1 (25.0)
25DK13	1 (7.1)	0	0	1 (7.1)	0	0	0	0	0	2 (14.3)	2 (14.3)	8 (57.1)

The Crow Creek female and male crania are correctly identified in 78.1 and 65.7 percent of the cases, respectively. This correct identification frequency is greater than any of the other groups except the Mandan, Omaha, and Pawnee--the other groups which tend to fall on the extremes of the first three CV's--and the Leavenworth males. Crow Creek's correct identification frequency probably should be expected because it fell on one extreme of CV I, the CV explaining the greatest amount of variability. Although the correction identifications are interesting, the pattern of incorrect identifications are even more useful.

Crow Creek crania generally misidentify as St. Helena (25DK9 and 25KD13) or early Arikara (Mobridge, Rygh, and Sully). One Crow Creek male, an exception to this generalization, is incorrectly identified as Pawnee. The hit-miss table supports what the CV analysis of the group centroids indicated: namely, Crow Creek is most similar to the St. Helena and early Arikara samples.

These results suggest that Crow Creek's morphological affiliations are closest to the St. Helena and early Arikara samples. Patrick Key (1983:92) suggests that the St. Helena samples used here and in his analysis are late in the St. Helena period, making them roughly contemporaneous with Crow Creek. Key further suggests that similarities between Crow Creek and these St. Helena samples result from interaction between the two groups, rather than an ancestorial-descendant relationship. The early Arikara samples, on the other hand, are considerably later in time than Crow Creek. It seems probable that the Crow Creek villagers were members of a Caddoan-speaking group, as the Arikara. Probably the descendants of the Crow Creek people or their close relatives would have been Arikara.

The relationship between the Arikara and the Pawnee is not clarified by this analysis. It is not until the CV III that Crow Creek and the Pawnee sample are associated, and when the first three CV's are displayed, Crow Creek and the Pawnee are some distance apart. In the hit-miss tables, only one Crow Creek male is misclassified as a Pawnee; no Crow Creek females are misclassified as Pawnee and no Pawnee males or females are misclassified as Crow Creek. Part of the problem may be the small sample of Pawnee which originate from two different sites. Further, no crania from the Lower Loup, thought to be predecessors of the Pawnee, are included in this analysis. Larger samples of Pawnee and the addition of Lower Loup crania should clarify this problem.

The discrete trait results are difficult to interpret. The descriptive statistics, including the number of observations absent and present, the percentage present, and the θ value, are in Table 30. The calculated morphological distances are in Table 31 and are shown in Fig. 7. The discrete traits indicate that Crow Creek is the most distinct of the samples. It is most similar to Leavenworth and Rygh, although these differ greatly from Crow Creek. On the other hand, the St. Helena sample is the most different from Crow Creek, the sample which is the most similar based on metric distances.

If the interpretations about the morphological affiliations are based solely on these discrete trait results, the Crow Creek sample would be very different from the St. Helena and Arikara samples. Yet, intuitively, the material appears similar to the Arikara crania we have studied. A major problem with the discrete trait distances is they are not as readily interpretable as the metric data.

Table 30. Number of discrete traits absent and present, percentage present, and θ-value for the combined sexes of Crow Creek.

Discrete Traits	Number Absent/Present	Percent Present	θ
Medial lambdoid ossicle	79/31	28.2	.45
Lateral lambdoid ossicle	88/22	20.0	.64
Parietal foramen	70/51	42.1	.16
Coronal ossicle	124/1	0.8	1.39
Epipteric bone	87/7	7.4	1.02
Ossicle in mastoid suture	82/22	21.2	.61
Anterior condylar canal double	100/26	20.6	.63
Accessory palatine foramen	12/97	89.0	-.89
Supraorbital foramen complete	82/48	36.9	.26
Frontal foramen	63/68	51.9	-.04
Accessory infraorbital foramen	92/22	19.3	.66
Accessory mental foramen	52/7	11.9	.87
Lambdoidal ossicle	52/7	11.9	.87
Inca bone	58/1	1.7	1.31
Pharyngeal fossa	45/18	28.6	.44
Superior sagittal sulcus turns left	45/18	28.6	.44

Table 31. Morphological distances based on 16 cranial discrete trait frequencies of Crow Creek and other samples.

	Leavenworth	Larson	Mobridge	Rygh	Sully	St. Helena
Crow Creek	.90	1.23	1.09	0.93	1.50	3.30
Leavenworth		.00	1.36	.00	1.22	0.81
Larson			.00	.00	2.16	0.12
Mobridge				.00	.02	0.16
Rygh					2.74	0.14
Sully						0.33

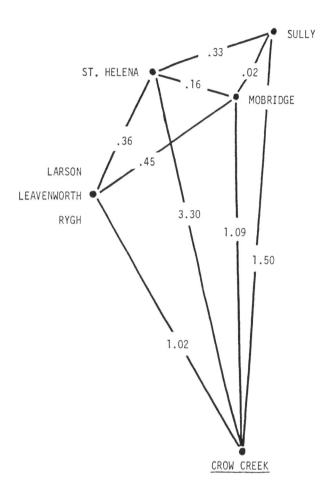

Figure 7. Morphological distances based on non-metric traits between Crow Creek and other cranial samples.

The meaning of discrete traits and their comparability to metrics has been much discussed in the literature (e.g., Carpenter 1976, Cheverud et al. 1979, Corruccini 1976). The purpose here is not to detail these discussions but to suggest reasons why the Crow Creek discrete trait and metric distances differ. The first possibility is that the CV's used to determine the metric distances is relatively sophisticated while the discrete trait statistic is fairly simple. Nevertheless it is hard to believe that the difference in statistical sophistication alone would account for such divergent results. Another possible explanation for the differences is that the discrete trait observations may be more susceptible to interobserver error. This error would tend to make samples artificially more dissimilar than they are in actuality. It is also possible that discrete traits lack the sensitivity of craniometrics, and uninterpretable results should be expected when populations as similar as those studied here are examined.

C. Summary

This chapter deals with variations within the Crow Creek sample and affinities between Crow Creek crania and other samples from the Northern and Central Plains.

Within the Crow Creek sample, two analyses are performed. Searching for craniometrically dissimilar skulls, an outlier analysis is performed employing principal component scores for the individuals and calculating D^2 from the group centroid. The results of the test indicate that no individuals differed from the group beyond the 0.05 probability level. It is concluded, then, that all of the measured skulls come from the same homogeneous group. The second analysis is performed to search for craniometric variation patterned by the skulls' east-west location in the ditch. Principal component scores for individuals are analyzed using discriminant analysis. No craniometric patterning based on location is present, so apparently the skulls were placed in the ditch without regard to cranial morphology and presumably without regard for kinship affiliation.

The other major purpose of this chapter is comparing Crow Creek with other cranial samples from the Plains to suggest affinities. Three approaches to among-group comparisons are made.

First, the raw craniometrics are converted into canonical variates (CV's). The first CV explains 35.7 and 43.1 percent of the female and male variability, respectively. CV I separates Crow Creek and to a lesser extent the St. Helena samples from the others. It also arranges the Arikara samples temporally and may be doing the same to the St. Helena samples and Crow Creek. CV II explains 33.3 and 24.3 percent of the female and male variability, respectively. This CV seems to be displaying geographic ordering. In CV II, Crow Creek is generally most similar to the St. Helena and earlier Arikara samples. The other two CV's (CV III and IV) explain much less variability and are less easily interpreted.

The second approach to comparing Crow Creek crania with other samples employs a hit-miss table. Crow Creek is a relatively homogeneous sample, correctly classifying about 70 percent of its own members. Those Crow Creek skulls which are misclassified are generally misidentified as St. Helena or early Arikara. From this approach as well as the CV analysis, it is concluded that the Crow Creek specimens are probably members of a Caddoan-speaking group whose descendants or their close relations became the Arikara.

The third approach employs cranial discrete traits to assess affinities. Crow Creek is most similar to an early and a late Arikara sample and least similar to St. Helena. These results are difficult to reconcile with the craniometric results. Because the craniometric results are interpretable and the discrete trait results are not, the craniometric results are emphasized over those of the discrete traits.

Chapter 6
Crow Creek Mutilations

There are many historic accounts telling stories of Plains Indian atrocities and mutilations. Many skirmishes and battles were recorded and some describe mutilations, usually done by Indians to Whites, although the reverse is also recorded.

The historic hostilities are often considered aberrant contrasted to the prehistoric conditions. It is frequently thought that historic aggression was caused by depopulation of the Indians, White intrusion forcing many Indian groups to move from their traditional territories, Whites propagating hostilities among Indian groups, and the introduction of new goods--especially horses and guns. In contrast the prehistoric conditions are thought to have been tranquil.

This idea may have been caused in part by the nature of the ambiguous prehistoric evidence. But deadmen do tell tales, even if their story is abbreviated, obscured by fickle preservation, and cryptic. Perhaps the biggest problem is that there are relatively few prehistoric skeletons available for study. Another problem is that identifying perimortem trauma from bones is difficult in the first place, and attributing trauma to interpersonal aggression is even more tenuous. And even when interpersonal aggression is indicated, determining whether the trauma occurred before and perhaps caused or contributed to death or was a mere mutation following death is usually impossible.

So when skeletal material comes from contexts indicating violence, careful inspection of the skeletons for perimortem trauma is warranted. There are only a few archaeological sites on the Plains where battles were fought.

Crow Creek is not the only or the earliest massacre archaeologically witnessed on the Northern or Central Plains. There are three other sites whose contexts suggest violent deaths. They are briefly described here in chronological order.

The Fay Tolton Site (39ST11) in central South Dakota dates approximately 1000-1100 AD (Wood 1976). Four people (an adult male, two adolescent females?, and a child) in House 1 appear to have been murdered as well as one (an adult male) in House 2 (Butler 1976:28-29). The hands of one of the adolescent females? may have been severed (Butler 1976:29) and one of the adult males may have been decapitated (Lehmer 1971:101). Although the skeletons have been described (Bass and Berryman 1976), no detailed inspection of the bones for mutilations has been made.

The Wright Site (25NC3) is in east-central Nebraska and probably dates between 1650 and 1700 AD (O'Shea 1980). The bodies of approximately 50 people were concentrated in a lodge near the entryway, and the lodge was burned (O'Shea 1980). This context has been interpreted as evidence that the people sought refuge in the lodge which was set ablaze, trapping and killing them. Apparently the skeletal remains have not been analyzed.

The Larson Village (39WW2) is in north-central South Dakota and may date approximately 1780 AD (Jantz 1972), although recent work suggests this date is too recent (O'Shea 1984). The remains of about 75 people were in three lodges, and the lodges were burned. Owsley et al. (1977) found that many of the skeletons were scalped, dismembered, and burned. Material from this site will be compared with the Crow Creek mutilations later in this chapter.

It is apparent from the three examples cited above that the violence at Crow Creek is not unique. There are indications of violence on the Plains predating Crow Creek by several centuries, and some of the same kinds of mutilations found at Crow Creek have also been described from the Larson Village material. What separates Crow Creek from the others is the enormous number of people killed, and the variety and frequency of the mutilations.

The prehistoric Crow Creek victims offer an excellent opportunity to identify conservatively perimortem trauma which marred their bones. The first purpose of this study is descriptive. A list of the mutilations observed and frequencies of certain kinds of mutilations are presented. The second purpose of this study is comparative. The mutilations on the Crow Creek ditch victims are compared with those found on the bones inside the ditch in the Crow Creek Village proper, those from the protohistoric Larson Village massacre, and the copious historic accounts from the Northern Plains. These comparisons permit tracing the continuity of some atrocities from the historic documents into the prehistoric period.

A. Material and Methods

About 1700 sacks of Crow Creek material were inspected, although some of the material from the looter's hole may have been omitted. A data collection form was used which listed the elements inspected and provided space for notes. The description of burned bones is based on their study by Mark Swegle (in Zimmerman et al. 1981:182-187); the other mutilations were examined by Willey.

To obtain a list of and an orientation to the variety of the mutilations present, a preliminary examination of 100 bags of material was made in February of 1979. All fragments in all 100 bags were inspected for perimortem damage, and the damages were noted on the inventory forms. Specifically the bones were inspected for cutting, old but unhealed breaks, and chewing. This procedure was extremely tedious and too time-consuming to complete in the time available for the study, so the process was modified. The rest of the bones were observed for a limited number of traits which were readily observable and could be recorded as present or absent. Other usual traits not consistently observed were noted, although frequency data for these features (e.g., postcranial cutting and burning) were not recorded. The rest of this description of the methods concentrates on those observations amenable to frequency data, beginning with the skull and proceeding inferiorly.

Skulls and mandibles were inspected for cuts, fractures, and evulsions. Cutting of the cranial vault was generally interpreted as scalping. The cut bones were noted on the mutilation inventory sheet. While inspecting the more complete skulls, it became apparent that the deepest cuts in the vaults almost always occur on the frontals, an observation supported by the historic accounts and previous descriptions of skeletal scalpings. The frequency of scalping was based on the presence and absence of the cuts on the frontal. Fragmentary frontals were included in the count only when more than half of the lateral portion of the frontal was present. In addition to the frequency of frontal scalping, note was made of all cranial bones with cuts. This inventory was intended to show the distribution of cuts on the skull vault, not the frequency of presence and absence.

Cuts on the base of the skull (near the foramen magnum, especially the occipital condyles) and the first and second cervical vertebrae were interpreted as decapitation. Occasionally cuts were noticed on the alveolar portion of the mandible and maxilla, and these were recorded, but no frequency data were taken.

After more than three-fourths of the bags had been inspected, cuts were found near the nasal aperture, suggesting nose cutting or face slicing; at that point an attempt was make to record the presence and absence of these cuts. Later, when the more complete skulls were removed from their sacks for a different analysis, their nasal apertures were also inspected for cuts. Thus some frequency data were available for this mutilation, although a complete inventory was not performed. Mandibles, especially the inferior and posterior borders, were inspected for cutting.

Fractures on the cranial vault were also noted. It was especially difficult with linear fractures to assess whether they happened near the time of death or much later. Because of this uncertainty, linear breaks were not noted, but only depressed fractures were systematically searched for. One hundred one relatively complete skulls were inspected by Max Schmeling, then a student at the University of South Dakota. The fractures' locations, shapes, sizes and axes were noted.

Evulsions were noted for both the maxilla and mandible. Generally the criteria used to determine the presence of evulsions were an old, stained color of the broken tooth surface or an irregularly broken tooth. In a few cases other criteria were used; if the alveolar portion surrounding a broken tooth root was snapped, the tooth was considered evulsed.

The presence and absence of cutting, fracturing, and evulsion were noted on the forms. In those cases where there was not enough of the specimen present for an assessment of presence or absence, a dash was put beside the appropriate heading. Recording mutilations present on the postcranial remains followed this same format, although the parts present were also noted.

When recording the postcranial mutilations, the part and portion of the long bones present was noted first. The part of the bone was listed as proximal, shaft, distal, or whole. Whole was used when both ends and the shaft were present, proximal when the proximal articular end was present, distal when the distal articular end was present, and shaft when neither end was present. The portion indicated how much of the specimen was present. Proportions were estimated and noted in the following fractions: 1/8's, 1/4's, 1/3's, and 1/2's.

Spaces were provided on the mutilation inventory form for almost all long bones. In all cases the proportion and part of the bone present were noted, followed by the condition of the ends. The missing ends were listed as being whole, chewed, splintered, or lost postmortem (example, "Dist. chewed").

Because chewing, splintering, and snapping are ambiguous terms, they require definition. Chewing was used to describe small puncture marks which were commonly found near the ends of the Crow Creek long bones and the projecting parts of other bones (Fig. 8). This designation was based on the similarities between these marks on the Crow Creek material and marks found on present-day forensic cases in the University of Tennessee collection. The present-day marks were attributed to dogs or coyotes chewing the bones. These marks are also similar to those reportedly produced by canid chewing (Miller 1975).

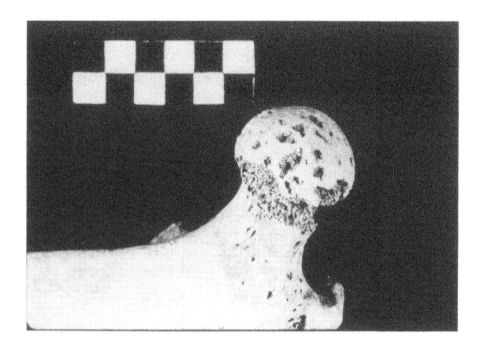

Figure 8. Chewing on left femur head. Scale in centimeters. Specimen 39BF11 70-12.

While inspecting the Crow Creek material, the use of chewing changed. As the data collection proceeded, broad grooves were noticed near some chewed ends. These grooves appeared to have been caused by gnawing with the posterior teeth rather than chewing with the anterior or chewing without marked penetration into the bone. In these instances chewing was used to describe the grooves although the characteristic puncture marks were absent.

Snapping was used when it appeared that the bone was broken by transverse pressure while it was fresh. In many instances a "hinge" fracture was present (Fig. 9). In the early stages of data collection, there was a tendency to identify more bones snapped than later. Many of the bones identified as snapped earlier in the data collection would have been identified as splintered after Box 50. To compensate for this change in methods, the snapped and splintered categories are combined for analytical purposes.

Splintering was when the bone end was not chewed or snapped but had a jagged projection or projections and the cortical surface of the break was smooth, apparently having happened while the bone was fresh (Fig. 10). Splintering may have resulted from direct pressure, especially with some tool or as the bone fell against some hard object. Some bones identified as splintered may actually have been chewed, but lack the identifying puncture marks or grooves. Crushing is similar to splintering but probably resulted from activity after the bone lost its viability; cortical break surfaces were rough.

In addition to the bones of the skull and neck and the long bones, short and irregular bones were inspected. The bones of the hands and feet were inspected and noted. Each of the few carpals recovered was individually inspected and noted. The tarsals, except the

Figure 9. Snapping of left humerus shaft. Scale in inches. Specimen 39WW2-932.

Figure 10. Splintering of long bones.

A.   Splintered distal radius (above) and ulna (below). Specimens 39BF11 137-7.

B.   Splintered distal femur shaft. Scale in centimeters. Specimen 39BF11 53-5.

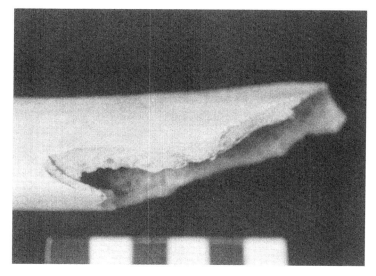

cuneiforms, were individually inspected; although not individually separated, the cuneiforms were inspected for mutilation.

The innominates were inspected for the presence and absence of chewing on the iliac crest and the ischium. In many instances of chewing on the iliac crest, the chewing centered near the anterior superior spine and this was noted.

Although there was not space provided on the recording sheets, presence and absence of chewing on patellae were also noted. No space was provided for the scapulae or clavicles either, but they were inspected too. On the scapula, only the acromial process was examined and note made whether the process was whole, chewed, or splintered. Clavicles were examined following the process described for the long bones, although the ends were listed as <u>medial</u> and <u>lateral</u> rather than <u>proximal</u> and <u>distal</u>.

Absences of mutilation were noted by the end of the bone being listed as present, but no indication of mutilation being noted. This was a potentially confusing, although expeditious, way of noting the lack of mutilation. Small fragments and those fragments lacking definitive modifications were omitted from inspection. Questionable assessments were followed by a question mark. Combinations of modifications were noted by listing both mutations with the first modification listed being the more pronounced or more likely.

To provide a visual record, photographs were taken of examples of each category. Some of the negatives have been lost, and those that remain are at the University of South Dakota. Because of their loss, one of the photographs presented in this study is of a skeletal element from the River Basin Survey's excavations of the Larson Village.

The methods used on the Crow Creek skeletons were also used to examine those from the Larson Village and the Nebraska State Historical Society's Crow Creek Village skeletons. Both samples were studied in January 1981.

Published historic sources were searched for descriptions of mutilations. First a few general sources concerning Plains warfare (e.g. Smith 1938) were used to locate primary sources. Then those primary sources dealing with the Northern Plains and adjacent areas were read and a search made of other likely sources available in the University of Tennessee's libraries. It should be noted that the library collections locally available were limited. While the search was somewhat eclectic and doubtlessly many valuable published sources were missed, the sample probably includes a representative list of historic mutilations, which was the purpose of this search.

B. Results and Discussion

Crow Creek Mutilations

The great majority of the Crow Creek frontals show cuts suggesting scalping. Of the frontals in Bed A, 17 (94.4 percent) are cut and one (5.6 percent) may have been (Table 32). In Bed B 354 (89.2 percent) are cut, 24 (8.1 percent) may have been, and 19 (4.8 percent) are not (Table 32). There is no age group or sex exempt from scalping: women and children as well as men display the distinctive cuts.

When the cuts observed on all cranial bones and fragments (Table 33) are tabulated by age (adult, adolescent, and child), there are statistically significant differences (Table 34) among the age groups and the bones cut ($X^2 = 12.90$, DF = 6, P < 0.05). Infants are

Table 32. Mutilations of skulls from Crow Creek. Percentages by bone bed and mutilation are in parentheses.

Multilations	Bone Bed A			Bone Bed B		
	Present	Present?	Absent	Present	Present?	Absent
Scalping	17 (94.4)	1 (5.6)	0	354 (89.2)	24 (4.8)	19 (6.0)
Cut Noses	0	0	0	4 (4.5)	0	85 (95.5)
Evulsions	3 (75.0)	1 (25.0)	0	35 (23.5)	7 (4.7)	107 (71.8)
Decapitation Occipital	2 (66.7)	0	1 (33.3)	31 (13.6)	6 (2.6)	191 (83.8)
Cervical 1	1 (100.0)	0	0	56 (24.5)	3 (1.3)	170 (74.2)
Cervical 2	0	0	0	31 (16.5)	4 (2.1)	153 (81.4)

Table 33. The location of cuts on the Crow Creek skulls and skull fragments suggesting scalping by age and sex. Both Beds A and B are included. Percentages by column are in parentheses.

Locations	Female	Female?	?	Male	Male?	Adolescent	Child	Infant	Total
Frontal									
High	42 (22.0)	35 (26.5)	40 (26.1)	31 (28.2)	24 (32.4)	24 (26.4)	77 (29.3)	8 (38.1)	281 (27.1)
Middle	0	0	3 (2.0)	4 (3.6)	2 (2.7)	2 (2.2)	8 (3.0)	0	19 (1.8)
Low	5 (2.6)	7 (5.3)	6 (3.9)	10 (9.1)	6 (8.1)	6 (6.6)	12 (4.6)	0	52 (5.0)
Total	17 (8.9)	11 (8.3)	10 (6.5)	5 (4.5)	1 (1.4)	5 (5.5)	8 (3.0)	1 (4.8)	58 (5.6)
	64 (33.5)	53 (40.1)	59 (38.5)	50 (45.4)	33 (44.6)	37 (40.7)	105 (39.9)	9 (42.9)	410 (39.5)
Parietal									
	1 (0.5)	1 (0.8)	7 (4.6)	1 (0.9)	0	3 (3.3)	26 (9.9)	1 (4.8)	40 (3.9)
Left	40 (20.9)	24 (18.2)	25 (16.3)	17 (15.5)	15 (20.3)	14 (15.4)	45 (17.1)	4 (19.0)	184 (17.8)
Right	37 (19.4)	22 (16.7)	31 (20.3)	18 (16.4)	12 (16.2)	13 (14.3)	47 (17.9)	4 (19.0)	184 (17.8)
Total	78 (40.8)	47 (35.7)	63 (41.2)	36 (32.8)	27 (36.5)	30 (33.0)	118 (44.9)	9 (42.8)	408 (39.5)
Temporal									
	0	0	2 (1.3)	1 (0.9)	1 (1.4)	1 (1.1)	1 (0.4)	0	6 (0.6)
Left	11 (5.8)	12 (9.1)	8 (5.2)	7 (6.4)	5 (6.8)	8 (8.8)	9 (3.4)	1 (4.8)	61 (5.9)
Right	11 (5.8)	8 (6.1)	9 (5.9)	6 (5.5)	2 (2.7)	4 (4.4)	5 (1.9)	0	45 (4.3)
Total	22 (11.6)	20 (15.2)	19 (12.4)	14 (12.8)	8 (10.9)	13 (14.3)	15 (5.7)	1 (4.8)	112 (10.8)
Occipital	27 (14.1)	12 (9.1)	12 (7.8)	10 (9.1)	6 (8.1)	11 (12.1)	25 (9.5)	2 (9.5)	105 (10.1)
Total	191 (100.0)	132 (100.1)	153 (99.9)	110 (100.1)	74 (100.1)	91 (100.1)	263 (100.0)	21 (100.0)	1035 (99.9)

Table 34. Comparison of Crow Creek cranial cuts by age. Infants are omitted because of small sample size.

Elements	Adults		Adolescents		Children	
	Expected	Observed	Expected	Observed	Expected	Observed
Frontal	261.0	259	36.0	37	104.0	105
Parietal	259.7	251	35.8	30	103.5	118
Temporal	72.2	83	10.0	13	28.8	15
Occipital	67.0	67	9.2	11	26.7	25

$X^2 = 12.904$, DF $= 6$, P < 0.05

omitted from this analysis because of small sample sizes. The largest differences from expected values are found in the lack of cut adult parietals and child temporals and the abundance of the cut adult temporals and child parietals.

If it is assumed that no differences in preservation or breakage exist among the age groups, then it appears that more of the scalp of adults and adolescents was taken, while only the top-lock of the scalp of children was removed. This distribution suggests several possible explanations. The hair on the sides of the children's heads may have been undesirable, or perhaps the scalp could be ripped more easily from their heads than that of adolescents and adults. It is also possible that the hair style of the children differed from those of the adolescents and adults; the children's hair may have been in a "Mohawk" style more frequently than their elders. Finally the differences may be caused by the children's temporals being proportionately smaller than their parietal when compared with adult bones. This difference in proportions is caused by ontogenetic vault growth differences. Being smaller, the temporals may have been less likely cut than the larger parietals.

Using just the subadult data, a statistically significant difference (Table 35) in distribution of cuts exists between adolescents and children ($X^2 = 8.98$, DF = 3, P < 0.05). Similar to the differences between adult and child cut locations, the largest differences from expected values are the lack of cut adolescent parietals and child temporals, and the abundance of cut adolescent temporals and child parietals. Possible explanations for these observations are the same as those for the adult-child differences.

When the adult scalp marks are divided by bone and sex (female and female? categories are combined as are male and male?), no statistically significant differences are

Table 35. Comparison of adolescent and child cranial cuts from Crow Creek.

Elements	Adolescents		Children	
	Expected	Observed	Expected	Observed
Frontal	36.5	37	105.5	105
Parietal	38.0	30	110.0	118
Temporal	7.2	13	20.8	15
Occipital	9.3	11	26.7	25

$X^2 = 8.983$, DF = 3, $P < 0.05$

observed (X^2 = 4.32, DF = 3, 0.25 > P > 0.10, Table 36). Also, there is no statistically significant difference between the side of the temporals and parietals cut when all age categories are lumped (Z = 0.0001, F (Z) = 0.50, P > 0.45).

The typical Crow Creek scalping has two elements: the primary, circling cuts and the secondary, scattered cuts. The circling begins with the deepest, most frequent cuts slicing traversely across the frontal midway between nasion and bregma. Sometimes the circling cuts are single and long, but usually there are several groups of short cuts. As the circling cuts proceed posteriorly, the cuts generally become fewer and shallower on the lateral and posterior parts of the vault. Crests, lines, and processes usually best display the cuts. These cuts, when present, are found on the squamosal portion, temporal line, and sometimes the mastoid of the temporal and the squamosal portion of the occipital.

In addition to these primary, circling cuts, there are often secondary cuts scattered over the vault. The most likely purpose of the secondary cuts was loosening and skinning the scalp within the boundaries scribed by the circling cuts. Usually these secondary cuts are in a transverse direction, but there is much variability.

Variations from the typical scalping just described were noted while inspecting the Crow Creek remains. One variation is the location of the primary cuts on the frontal. These cuts usually are present midway on the frontal, but sometimes they are located lower on the frontal, in some cases immediately superior to glabella. At the other extreme, some cuts begin near bregma.

A second variation is present on some occipitals. Occasionally the circling cuts on the posterior portion of the vault are much inferior to inion. These cuts must have severed the

Table 36. Comparison of female and male cranial cuts from Crow Creek. Female and female?, and male and male? categories are combined.

Elements	Female		Male	
	Expected	Observed	Expected	Observed
Frontal	127.4	117	72.6	83
Parietal	119.8	125	68.2	63
Temporal	40.8	42	23.2	22
Occipital	35.0	39	20.0	16

$X^2 = 4.315$, DF = 3, $0.25 > P > 0.10$

posterior nuchal muscles. Because these cuts are some distance from the foramen magnum, they probably do not indicate decapitation. Although it is assumed here that these cuts are associated with scalping, they might have been intended to mutilate the body otherwise.

A final variation is associated with some depressed fractures. When present, the primary cuts occur on the side of the fracture where the majority of the scalp was. This pattern suggests that the scalper was attempting to avoid gashes and punctures in the scalp, just as one might avoid a hole in a pelt. It also suggests that the fractures--at least in some cases--happened before the scalping.

There are other possible indications of scalping besides the cut marks just discussed. Some historic accounts (e.g., Catlin 1844:238) tell that some people lived through the scalping ordeal. At Crow Creek two skulls (numbers 13 and 264) show remodeling comparable to what has been identified as survival following scalping (Hamperl and Laughlin 1959). Neither of these two skulls retain any cut marks, the marks apparently having been remodeled and destroyed. The importance of these two skulls is that they indicate the violence was not limited to the Crow Creek massacre itself but was more long-lived, at least a matter of months if not years.

That nearly 90 percent of the skulls show indications of scalping is all the more remarkable when two things are considered. First, the two skulls which appear to have been victims of previous scalping who survived until the massacre are omitted from the count of those skulls with cut marks and consequently not included with those scalped. Second, Hamperl (1967) demonstrated that it was possible to scalp a person and leave no marks on the bone. So the frequency of cut frontals must be considered a minimum; the actual frequency of scalping may well have approached 100 percent.

About 40 percent of the skulls have depressed fractures (Table 37). Most of the fractured skulls had one depressed fracture, although two skulls had as many as five. The majority of the fractures (Table 38) were on the parietals, fewer on the frontals, nearly none on the occipital, and none at all on the temporals. Bluntly speaking, the blows were most common on the top of the vaults, least common on the sides and base.

The outline of the more complete depressions is either round or ellipsoid. Of the 66 depressed fractures classified as round or ellipsoid, 22 (33.3 percent) are round (Fig. 11) and 44 (66.7 percent) are ellipsoid (Fig. 12). There are both large and small round depressed fractures. While in some cases the ellipsoid fractures may have been caused by an instrument with a round diameter obliquely striking the skull, in other instances it is apparent that the tool used had an axe-like cross-section. These ellipsoid depressions, when the depressed bone plug is left intact, have a linear crack running the long axis of the ellipsoid as well as the oval crack forming the outline of the ellipsoid fracture (Fig. 12). No hatchets with cross-sections like this have been recovered archaeologically from this time period in the Middle Missouri Region (R. Alex 1979).

Only four (4.5 percent) of the 89 nasal apertures inspected are cut (Table 32). Those few cuts present are immediately lateral and parallel to the long axis of the nose, although one cut is present immediately inferior to the nasal sill. It is unfortunate that more cuts were not found so a more definitive pattern could be established.

Table 37. Skulls with and without depressed fractures from Crow Creek. Percentages are in parentheses.

Skulls with Fractures Number of Fractures per Skull					Skulls without Fractures
1	2	3	4	5	
28	8	2	2	2	
(66.7)	(19.0)	(4.8)	(4.8)	(4.8)	
Total count		42			59
		(41.6)			(58.4)

Table 38. Location of depressed fractures on Crow Creek skulls.

Quantity	Frontal	Parietal		Occipital	Temporal
		Left	Right		
Number	20	18	27	3	0
Percentage	29.4	26.5	39.7	4.4	

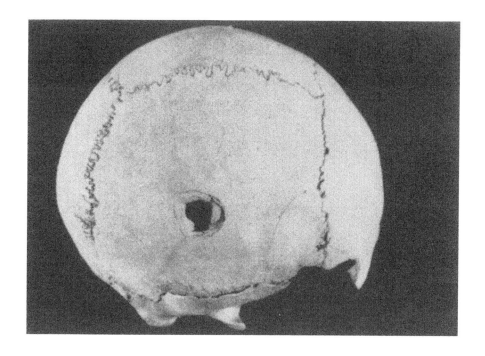

Figure 11. Round depressed fracture on right parietal. Hole diameter 12mm. Specimen 39BF11 98-16 Skull 230.

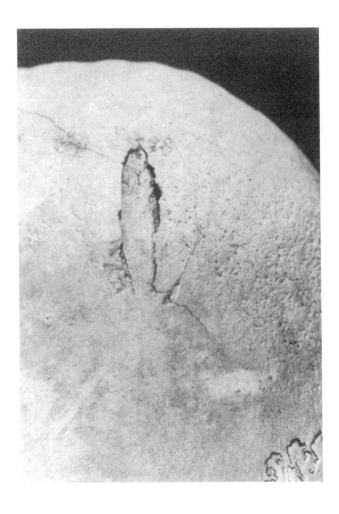

Figure 12. Ellipsoid depressed fracture on left parietal. Length of fracture 35mm. Specimen 39BF11 96-1 Skull 216.

Evulsion or removal of the teeth occurs fairly frequently among the Crow Creek specimens (Table 32). There are three (75.0 percent) with and one (25.0 percent) possibly without the evulsions in Bed A. Bed B showed the reverse portions: namely, 35 (23.5 percent) with, 107 (71.8 percent) without, and the rest (7 or 4.7 percent) are questionable.

Tongues may have been cut from the mouths of the Crow Creek victims. Cuts on the posterior border of the ascending ramus of the mandible may have been incidentally made by a knife during decapitation, but cuts on the inferior border of the corpus are harder to interpret this way. And even more difficult to include as part of beheading are cuts on the medial surface of the mandibular corpus. The most reasonable explanation for these marks is that some tongues were cut loose beginning in the throat under the chin rather than entering the mouth passing between the lips. Certainly this pattern was noted in historic accounts of bison butchering. Wheat (1972:103) summarizes the historic accounts of bison butchering in this way, "The tongue could be removed at any point during the butchering, ordinarily by slitting the skin between the angles of the mandibles, pulling the tongue downward through the slit, and cutting it off." Some of the cuts found on the Crow Creek mandibles may have resulted from a comparable manner of tongue severing. Tongue removal as well as decapitation and dismemberment of the Crow Creek victims may well have been based on standard aboriginal butchering practices of large game animals.

Decapitation is indicated by cuts around the foramen magnum and on cervical vertebrae 1 (C-1) and 2 (C-2). The frequency of these cuts is presented in Table 32. Because few observations are possible on material from Bed A, comments are confined to those from Bed B. Cuts are most common on C-1. If this frequency can be taken as an accurate reflection of decapitation attempts, then at least a quarter (24.5 percent) were mutilated in this way.

The frequency of decapitation cuts varies depending on the bone. Dividing the cuts into those on the occipital, C-1, and C-2 and by presence, presence?, and absence ($X^2 = 10.22$, DF = 4, P < 0.05, Table 39) and by presence and absence alone ($X^2 = 9.17$, DF = 2, P < 0.025, Table 40), both display statistically significant relationships. The cells contributing most to significance are the relative under-representation of occipital cuts and the over-representation of C-1 cuts. This pattern suggests that the cuts in beheading attempts were centered around C-1, near the base of the skull.

The cuts near the foramen magnum tend to be anterior to the foramen on the condyles or lateral to the foramen magnum on the lateral portions of the occipital. Cuts on C-1 and C-2 tend to be on the anterior surfaces of the transverse processes. This pattern of cutting from anterior to posterior would avoid the problems of getting a blade between the spinous processes on the posterior portion of the vertebrae, but starting the cuts on the anterior surfaces would be difficult because the spaces between the bones would be hard to locate. The anterior to posterior cutting sequence during beheading attempts is similar to the scalping process.

There appears to be a preference for cutting one side during decapitation. Analyzing the cut occipitals and first two cervical vertebrae from both beds at Crow Creek, the right side of those elements are more frequently cut than the left ($Z = 2.2$, F (Z) = 0.9861, P < 0.014). It is difficult to reconcile these results with the scalping data which indicated no

Table 39. Comparison of Crow Creek decapitation cuts by element including uncertains. Specimens from Bed A are omitted because of small sample size.

Elements	Present		Absent		Uncertain	
	Expected	Observed	Expected	Observed	Expected	Observed
Occipital	41.7	31	181.7	191	4.6	6
Cervical 1	41.9	56	182.5	170	4.6	3
Cervical 2	34.4	31	149.8	153	3.8	4

$X^2 = 10.22$, DF = 4, $P < 0.05$

Table 40. Comparison of Crow Creek decapitation cuts by element excluding uncertains. Specimens from Bed A are omitted.

Elements	Present		Absent	
	Expected	Observed	Expected	Observed
Occipital	41.4	31	180.6	191
Cervical 1	42.2	56	183.8	170
Cervical 2	34.4	31	149.6	153

$X^2 = 9.17$, DF = 2, P < 0.025

significant side preference. Apparently the two mutilations were performed separately or in an unrelated manner.

There are other cuts which may indicate beheading. Cuts are present on the posterior border of the mandibular ascending ramus, the gonial angle, and the inferior border of the corpus. These cuts on the mandible may be indications of decapitation attempts. Because of the disarticulation at Crow Creek, no association between the cuts on the mandible, occipital, and first two cervical vertebrae can be established. It is, nevertheless, a possibility.

Besides decapitation, other dismemberments are suggested by cuts on other postcranial bones. This discussion starts with cuts on the bones of the arm, then proceeds inferiorly to those of the leg. It should be recalled that no specific search was made for these cuts, and those noticed are probably only the most obvious ones.

Cuts are present on all three of the elements of the arm and forearm. Starting proximally and proceeding distally, three cuts are located on the proximal portion of the humerus (Box 41-Bag 6, 117-12, 158-9), a possible cut near midshaft (22-2-D), and two near the distal end of the humerus (60-10, 150-3). All but one of the cuts are on right humeri. There are three cuts on ulnae: two near the proximal end (23-9, 74-7) and one near the distal end (164-14). One radius (71-12-A) has a cut one-third of the bone's length from the distal end of the anterior surface.

There are a number of Crow Creek bones from the lower appendages which suggest dismemberment. An innominate (29-16) is cut on the lateral surface of the ilium. The only other cuts found near the hip are on the medial surface of the proximal ends of six femora (125-1, 129-5, 134-7, 151-12-C, 156-1-A, 166-12-A-B). All except one of the cuts (125-1) are on right femora. A right tibia (164-3) and a right? fibula (51-6-A-C) are cut on the proximal ends.

When all of the cut long bones are considered together, there is an interesting difference in incidence by side (Table 41). Almost four times more rights are cut than lefts. Assuming that cutting is equally probable on each side and the sides are equally represented, the distribution of cuts is statistically significant ($Z = 2.52$, $F(Z) = 0.9941$, $P < 0.01$). But because it has been established from the minimum count presented in a previous chapter that rights ($n = 1737$) are more frequent than lefts ($n = 1653$), the second assumption is violated. Lefts amount to 95.7 percent of the right total, and the probability of randomly drawing a left from the sideable bones of the Crow Creek is 0.4876, a right is 0.5124. Using these revised probabilities, the cutting distribution is still significant ($Z = 2.42$, $F(Z) = 0.9922$, $P < 0.01$), so the distribution is not due to the over-representation of the right side. What this distribution means is problematic.

If, as appears to be the case in the present data, rights are more often cut and rights presumably more frequently severed from the trunk and thus more subject to loss, then we would expect right elements to be less common than the lefts--the reverse of what is observed. It is possible that the right side of the body, tending to have more muscles and tissues, required more cutting than the left, thus leaving more cuts on the right. It is of interest that the major left-right differences in cutting frequency are on the more proximal limb bones--the humerus and femur--which have greater muscle mass than the distal limb bones. These results are as would be expected according to the explanation presented. Admittedly this explanation is tenuous.

Table 41. Number of Crow Creek long bones with cuts.

Elements	Left	Right	Total
Humerus	1	5	6
Ulna	2	1	3
Radius	0	1	1
Femur	1	6	7
Tibia	0	1	1
Fibula	0	1	1
Total	4	15	19

Besides the presence of cutting, it is possible that some of the splintered and snapped bones may indicate dismemberment. Some of the limb bones may have been smashed, then a cut made through the tissue and shattered bone fragments, severing the distal member from the body. Rather than attempting to locate and cut through the joints, shattering the bone near the appendage to be removed may have sped and facilitated the dismemberment. There is some slight support for this possibility because nearly all limbs are more frequently snapped or splintered at the distal end than the proximal, the humerus being the only exception (Table 42).

If snapping and splintering can indeed be considered caused by shattering blows and part of dismemberment, then toes, as indicated by snapped or splintered metatarsals, were most frequently severed (Table 43). Arms (acromial processes) were next most frequently dismembered, followed by fingers, hands, ankles, and feet, lower legs, and lower arms (Tables 42 and 43). It would be interesting to compare these observations statistically with postcranial cut marks to further test the assumption that some snapping and splintering was involved with dismemberment, but there are so few cuts observed (n = 19) that no reliable conclusions can be established. A major problem is whether all snapping and splintering was caused by shattering blows or caused by other processes.

It is possible that if the bones were thrown into the ditch, impact caused some bones to break, but it is entirely possible that much of the snapping and splintering was produced by scavengers chewing the bones. This possibility is especially likely for some of the small tubular bones, as the metatarsals and metacarpals, and some of the more cortical areas, as

Table 42. Crow Creek long bone modifications from Bed B. Questionable identifications are omitted. Numbers in parentheses are percentages for that bone.

Elements	Snapped and Chewed		Splintered		Crushed		Not Modified		Total	
Humerus										
Proximal	50	(4.2)	83	(7.0)	4	(0.3)	214	(18.1)	351	(29.6)
Shaft	1	(0.1)	24	(2.0)	0		384	(32.4)	409	(34.5)
Distal	168	(14.2)	82	(6.9)	4	(0.3)	170	(14.4)	424	(35.8)
Total	219	(18.5)	189	(15.9)	8	(0.6)	768	(64.9)	1184	(99.9)
Radius										
Proximal	27	(5.0)	28	(5.2)	2	(0.4)	129	(24.0)	186	(34.6)
Shaft	0		24	(4.5)	2	(0.4)	158	(29.4)	184	(34.2)
Distal	17	(3.2)	86	(15.9)	0		65	(12.1)	168	(31.2)
Total	44	(8.2)	138	(25.6)	4	(0.8)	352	(65.4)	538	(100.0)
Ulna										
Proximal	75	(12.8)	52	(8.9)	7	(1.2)	86	(14.7)	220	(37.5)
Shaft	2	(0.3)	32	(5.5)	1	(0.2)	176	(30.0)	211	(36.0)
Distal	13	(2.2)	76	(12.9)	1	(0.2)	66	(11.2)	156	(26.5)
Total	90	(15.3)	160	(27.3)	9	(1.6)	328	(55.9)	587	(100.1)
Femur										
Proximal	250	(12.7)	36	(1.8)	11	(0.6)	373	(18.9)	670	(34.0)
Shaft	7	(0.4)	14	(0.7)	0		629	(31.8)	650	(32.9)
Distal	183	(9.3)	169	(8.6)	13	(0.7)	291	(14.7)	656	(33.3)
Total	440	(22.4)	219	(11.1)	24	(1.3)	1293	(65.4)	1976	(100.2)
Tibia										
Proximal	69	(5.1)	102	(7.5)	8	(0.6)	273	(20.0)	452	(33.2)
Shaft	4	(0.3)	49	(3.6)	3	(0.2)	413	(30.3)	469	(34.4)
Distal	87	(6.4)	125	(9.2)	9	(0.7)	222	(16.3)	443	(32.6)
Total	160	(11.8)	276	(20.3)	20	(1.5)	908	(66.6)	1364	(100.2)
Fibula										
Proximal	5	(0.7)	30	(4.5)	0		175	(26.0)	210	(31.2)
Shaft	0		23	(3.4)	1	(0.1)	219	(32.5)	243	(36.0)
Distal	29	(4.3)	62	(9.2)	3	(0.4)	127	(18.8)	221	(32.7)
Total	34	(5.0)	115	(17.1)	4	(0.5)	521	(77.3)	674	(99.9)

Table 43. Modifications of non-long, postcranial bones from Crow Creek. Questionable identifications are omitted. Numbers in parentheses are percentages for that bone or feature.

Locations	Chewed		Snapped and Splintered		Not Modified		Total	
Acromial process	55	(40.1)	47	(34.3)	35	(25.5)	137	(999)
Sternum	4	(10.3)	0		35	(89.7)	39	(1000)
Sacrum	15	(15.3)	0		83	(84.7)	98	(1000)
Patella	14	(35.0)	0		26	(65.0)	40	(1000)
Iliac crest	138	(33.7)	1	(0.2)	271	(66.1)	410	(1000)
Ischium	143	(35.7)	0		258	(64.3)	401	(1000)
Carpals	2	(2.7)	0		72	(97.3)	74	(1000)
Metacarpals	3	(6.1)	11	(22.4)	35	(71.4)	49	(999)
Hand phalanges								
Proximal row	4	(16.0)	0		21	(84.0)	25	(1000)
Middle row	0		0		5	(100.0)	5	(1000)
Distal row	0		0		4	(100.0)	4	(1000)
Talus	38	(29.0)	0		93	(71.0)	131	(1000)
Calcaneous	79	(79.8)	0		20	(20.2)	99	(1000)
Other tarsals	8	(3.2)	0		241	(96.8)	249	(1000)
Metatarsals	40	(18.3)	110	(50.2)	69	(31.5)	219	(1000)
Foot phalanges								
Proximal row	1	(14.3)	1	(14.3)	5	(71.4)	7	(1000)

the acromial process. The more cancellous bones, on the other hand, are more likely to show the definitive tooth marks indicating chewing.

There are many bones which were chewed. The most common bones having puncture marks are the projections of cancellous bones and the ends of long bones. Chewing occurs most frequently on the calcaneus, followed by the acromial process, ischium, patella, iliac crest, and talus (Table 43). If some of the snapped or splintered bones were actually chewed, then metacarpals and metatarsals should be added to the list of frequently chewed bones.

The ends of long bones (Table 42) are commonly chewed, although less frequently than the bones already mentioned. The long bones most frequently chewed are the femur, humerus, ulna, and tibia. Even on these long bones, the shaft is virtually ignored in favor of chewing the ends of the bone. If snapping and splintering can be considered caused by chewing, then a distribution somewhat similar to the tooth marks is observed on the long bones (Table 42). The shafts are at least as frequently snapped or splintered as they are chewed.

It was noted above that the missing hands and feet may have been taken by the raiders, but it is also possible that these parts were devoured by the scavengers. The chewing on the bones of the hands, feet, lower arms, and lower legs testify to this suggestion.

From these observations, it is apparent that there was much chewing of the bodies, even if only the puncture marks are considered. This amount of chewing suggests that the bodies were exposed for some time before interment or that there were many scavengers present. Probably there was both a lapse of time and a great number of scavengers present.

The most likely scavengers responsible were the village dogs and the ubiquitous wolves and coyotes. Although no indications were found on the bones, it is also likely that the carrion-feeding birds were involved.

It is entirely possible that as large as the canids were and as small as an infant is that the bodies of some of the infants and small children may have been completely devoured by the scavengers (cf. Miller 1975:213) or dragged elsewhere, scattered, and not recovered for burial. If scavengers did remove the smaller bodies, then they would have affected the Crow Creek paleodemographic profile presented in Chapter 4.

Present-day field observations of canid scavenging should be mentioned here to flesh-out the picture of the scavenging process. All observations are presented in Miller (1975:212-213). When scavenging a large animal, the coyote first chews off the ear, then tears off the mandible. Next it concentrates on the internal organs. Then the parts of the bones which are readily accessible, especially the relatively cancellous ones, are attacked. These bones include the long bone ends and the calcaneus. Variations among coyotes as well as between episodes involving the same coyote from the ideal presented above are noted. While scavenging practices of other species doubtlessly differ, the fundamentals are probably similar. The Crow Creek bones follow the general pattern just described. The long bone ends and other cancellous projecting bones were chewed. On the other hand, as might be expected, there are a few indications of chewed ears or mandibles present at Crow Creek.

It is interesting that at least some scavengers concentrate on the internal organs before the bones. This suggests that perhaps before many of the Crow Creek bones were chewed that most of the internal organs had been consumed. The consumption of the nearly 500 Crow Creek viscera by scavengers would have required a great number of scavengers or a lengthy period of exposure or both.

The burned human bone was observed and reported by Mark Swegle (in Zimmerman et al. 1981:184-187). He reports that all observed burning was relatively light; the remains were charred but not calcined. At least seven individuals were charred: three adults, three adolescents, and a child. Of the seven charred skulls, all appeared to have been scalped before being burned. Various postcranial bones were charred. Usually when long bones were burned, it was the distal end of the fragment which was charred.

Crow Creek Village Mutilations

In addition to the human bones recovered in the fortification ditch, there are a few bones from Kivett's excavation in the Crow Creek Village. The small number of bones recovered allows only tentative comparisons with those from the fortification ditch. The mutilations on the village bones are presented as counts in Table 44. Although these numbers in some cases differ markedly from those found among the Crow Creek fortification ditch sample, these differences are probably due to the extremely small sample size of the Crow Creek Village collection. It is also possible that the village skeletal remains were less accessible both to mutilation and recovery or were mutilated in a manner which precluded recovery for reburial.

Table 44. Crow Creek Village postcranial modifications. Bones are from Kivett's excavation in the village proper.

Location	Chewed	Snapped and Splintered	Not Modified	Total
Clavicle				
Medial	0	0	1	1
Shaft	0	0	4	4
Lateral	2	0	2	4
Total	2	0	7	9
Humerus				
Proximal	0	0	1	1
Shaft	0	0	1	1
Distal	0	0	0	0
Total	0	0	2	2
Femur				
Proximal	0	0	3	3
Shaft	0	0	2	2
Distal	0	0	2	2
Total	0	0	7	7
Tibia				
Proximal	0	0	1	1
Shaft	0	0	2	1
Distal	0	0	1	1
Total	0	0	4	3
Fibula				
Proximal	0	0	0	0
Shaft	0	0	2	2
Distal	0	0	1	1
Total	0	0	3	3
Acromial process	0	0	1	1
Patella	1	0	0	1
Iliac crest	1	0	2	3
Ischium	0	0	2	2
Talus	0	0	1	1
Metatarsals	0	3	0	3

Larson Village Mutilations

There are many similarities between the kinds of mutilations observed on the prehistoric Crow Creek massacre victims' bones and the protohistoric Larson Village victims, but the frequencies of occurrence often differ. First the variety of mutilations is considered, then the frequencies.

Virtually all mutilations observed at Crow Creek are also present at Larson (Table 45), including scalping, evulsion, depressed fractures, and cuts on C-1 and C-2. Unlike Crow Creek, there are no cuts on the occipital or around the nose in the Larson Village sample. If cut noses are as uncommon at Larson Village as they are at Crow Creek, perhaps the Larson Village sample size is too small to detect the mutilation. The absence of decapitation cuts on the Larson occipitals, however, is surprising. The Larson sample size seems adequate; perhaps the use of metal knives or a better knowledge of human anatomy enabled the mutilators to avoid the occipital during decapitation. Another possibility is that the locus of decapitation is lower by the protohistoric period, perhaps centering on the lower cervicals. As the Crow Creek limb bones, the Larson Village bones are frequently chewed, splintered and snapped, crushed, and burned (Tables 46 and 47).

Turning to the frequencies of these mutilations, the two sites differ dramatically. With a single exception, the mutilations are more frequent at Crow Creek than Larson Village. The most likely explanation for this difference is that the Larson lodges as they burned collapsed on the bodies and permitted limited access and mutilation. It is also possible that some non-murdered bodies are included in the Larson Village sample, and these would diminish the frequencies even more. The single exception to the generalization that

Table 45. Mutilations of skulls from Larson Village. Percentages are in parentheses.

Mutilations	Present		Absent	
Scalping	12	(37.5)	20	(62.5)
Cut noses	0		35	(100.0)
Evulsions	6	(10.0)	54	(90.0)
Decapitations				
Occipital	0		34	(100.0)
C-1	2	(4.8)	40	(95.2)
C-2	3	(7.5)	37	(92.5)
Depressed fractures	5	(22.7)	17	(87.3)

Table 46. Larson Village long bone modifications. Questionable identifications omitted. Numbers in parentheses are percentages for that bone.

Locations	Chewed		Snapped and Splintered		Crushed		Smoked		Not Modified		Total	
Clavicle												
Medial	2	(0.9)	3	(1.3)	0		0		74	(31.9)	79	(34.1)
Shaft	0		0		0		1	(0.4)	82	(35.3)	83	(35.7)
Lateral	9	(3.9)	5	(2.2)	0		2	(0.9)	54	(23.3)	70	(30.3)
Total	11	(4.8)	8	(3.5)	0		3	(1.3)	210	(90.5)	232	(100.1)
Humerus												
Proximal	1	(0.4)	0		0		4	(1.4)	84	(29.6)	89	(31.4)
Shaft	0		3	(1.1)	0		0		101	(35.6)	104	(36.7)
Distal	9	(3.2)	0		0		7	(2.5)	75	(26.4)	91	(32.1)
Total	10	(3.6)	3	(1.1)	0		11	(3.9)	260	(91.6)	284	(100.2)
Radius												
Proximal	1	(0.4)	1	(0.4)	0		0		86	(34.1)	88	(34.9)
Shaft	0		0		0		1	(0.4)	89	(35.3)	90	(35.7)
Distal	0		4	(1.6)	0		3	(1.2)	67	(26.6)	74	(29.4)
Total	1	(0.4)	5	(2.0)	0		4	(1.6)	242	(96.0)	252	(100.0)
Ulna												
Proximal	4	(1.6)	3	(1.2)	0		2	(0.8)	77	(31.4)	86	(35.0)
Shaft	0		1	(0.4)	0		1	(0.4)	85	(34.7)	87	(35.5)
Distal	0		7	(2.9)	0		1	(0.4)	64	(26.1)	72	(29.4)
Total	4	(1.6)	11	(4.5)	0		4	(1.6)	226	(92.2)	245	(99.9)
Femur												
Proximal	12	(3.8)	0		1	(0.3)	1	(0.3)	91	(28.8)	105	(33.2)
Shaft	0		0		0		0		112	(35.4)	112	(35.4)
Distal	8	(2.5)	5	(1.6)	0		4	(1.3)	82	(25.9)	99	(31.3)
Total	20	(6.3)	5	(1.6)	1	(0.3)	5	(1.6)	285	(90.1)	316	(99.9)
Tibia												
Proximal	4	(1.5)	1	(0.4)	0		1	(0.4)	87	(31.9)	93	(34.2)
Shaft	0		1	(0.4)	0		0		93	(34.1)	94	(34.5)
Distal	6	(2.2)	3	(1.1)	0		1	(0.4)	76	(27.8)	86	(31.5)
Total	10	(3.7)	5	(1.9)	0		2	(0.8)	256	(93.8)	273	(100.2)
Fibula												
Proximal	1	(0.4)	7	(2.5)	0		1	(0.4)	79	(28.5)	88	(31.8)
Shaft	0		1	(0.4)	0		0		97	(35.0)	98	(35.4)
Distal	4	(1.4)	11	(4.0)	0		1	(0.4)	75	(27.0)	91	(32.8)
Total	5	(1.8)	19	(6.9)	0		2	(0.8)	251	(90.5)	227	(100.0)

Table 47. Modifications of non-long, postcranial bones from the Larson Village. Questionable identifications omitted. Numbers in paretheses are percentages for that bone.

Locations	Chewed		Snapped and Splintered		Smoked		Not Modified		Total	
Acromial process	4	(6.6)	4	(6.6)	3	(4.9)	50	(82.0)	61	(100.1)
Sternum	0		0		0		24	(100.0)	24	(100.0)
Sacrum	4	(14.3)	0		0		24	(85.7)	28	(100.0)
Patella	6	(12.5)	0		1	(2.1)	41	(85.4)	48	(100.0)
Iliac Crest	13	(16.0)	0		0		68	(84.0)	81	(100.0)
Ischium	7	(9.3)	0		0		68	(90.7)	75	(100.0)
Carpals	1	(0.6)	0		3	(1.7)	174	(97.8)	178	(100.0)
Metacarpals	9	(3.9)	4	(1.7)	6	(2.6)	214	(91.8)	233	(100.0)
Hand phalanges										
Proximal row	2	(1.2)	1	(0.6)	4	(2.3)	164	(95.9)	171	(100.0)
Middle row	0		1	(0.8)	1	(0.8)	117	(98.3)	119	(99.9)
Distal row	0		0		0		76	(100.0)	76	(100.0)
Talus	10	(12.2)	0		1	(1.2)	71	(86.6)	82	(100.0)
Calcaneous	7	(10.8)	0		0		58	(89.2)	65	(100.0)
Other tarsals	1	(0.4)	0		3	(1.2)	252	(98.4)	256	(100.0)
Metatarsals	3	(1.0)	4	(1.3)	5	(1.6)	298	(96.1)	310	(100.0)
Foot phalanges										
Proximal row	0		2	(1.1)	0		175	(98.9)	177	(100.0)
Middle row	0		0		0		63	(100.0)	63	(100.0)
Distal row	0		0		0		59	(100.0)	59	(100.0)

mutilations are more frequent at Crow Creek than Larson Village is burning. This fact supports the assertion that the bodies were concealed by the collapsed lodges and were relatively inaccessible.

<u>Historic Mutilations</u>

Atrocities are frequently recorded in historic accounts of Indian encounters. Unlike the quantitative comparison of Crow Creek with the Larson Village material, comparing the Crow Creek mutilations with historically recorded depredations must deal primarily with a list of mutilations. Frequencies of mutilations are rarely available, and those more fully described atrocities (e.g., surgeons' autopsies) generally involved only a small number of victims. Consequently historic accounts are used to suggest the diversity of mutilations, not the frequencies.

In this analysis the presentation of mutilations follows that used to describe those from Crow Creek: the comparison begins with the head, then proceeds inferiorly. But before presenting the body of descriptions, it is useful to mention some of the additional problems with the historic accounts and some of the accounts not used.

Many of the historic accounts are too vague to be used in the study. There are many examples. Corpses are described as "butchered" (Coues 1897:262), "mangled" (Boller 1959; Bryant and Murch 1864:115, 415, 498; Coleson 1977:55; Lowie 1935:230; Kane cited in Ewers 1967:135; Palmer 1887:3; Vaughn 1963:97, 98), "cut" (Dorsey 1881:332; Eastman 1849:156; Grinnel 1892:254), "disfigured" (Bryant and Murch 1864:206), "maimed" (Bryant and Murch 1864:115), or just plain "mutilated" (Bryant and Murch 1864:103, 115, 140, 440;

Boyd 1925:8; Coleson 1977:22; Coues 1897:260; David 1937:219; Denig 1928-29:429; DeSmet 1904, v. 27:185; Dorsey 1881:313; Spring 1969:93; Vaughn 1963:94). These statements are interesting because they do indicate mutilations, but for our purposes more specific descriptions are needed.

Of the more specific listings of mutilations, scalping is the best known. It is frequently described in historic accounts of Plains battles. Descriptions of scalpings include Boller (1959:151; 1966:203-206), Bryant and Murch (1864:206, 219, 251, 253, 328, 363-364, 394), Camp (1976:95, 237, 248), Coleson (1977:22, 23), Coues (1897:262), David (1937:127, 145, 215, 219), Denig (1928-29:491-492), Eastman (1849:156), Godfrey (1974:112), Luttig (1964:124), Paulding (1974:10-11), Spring (1969:92), and Springer (1971:44, 52). Audubon (1897, v. 2:5) even describes an incident when a woman was scalped by Arikaras, later buried, then dug up and scalped again!

Scalping was systematic and patterned according to at least some sources. Adair's (1775:387-388) description of scalping in the Southeast is explicit.

> They seize the head of the disabled, or dead person, and placing one of their feet on the neck, they with one hand twist in the hair, extend it as far as they can--with the other hand, the barbarous artists speedily draw their long-pointed scalping knife out of a sheath from their breast, give a slash round the top of the skull and with a few dexterous scoops, soon strip it off. They are so expeditious as to take off a scalp in two minutes.

If Adair's statement that a scalp could be removed in two minutes is correct, then the approximately 360 scalps taken at Crow Creek would have required 12 work-hours for removal. Twelve work-hours should be considered a minimum because of the number of scalped Crow Creek skulls is a minimum count and probably two minutes to remove a scalp should be considered a minimum amount of time. It is likely that the actual time spent scalping the Crow Creek victims was more than 12 work-hours.

Larimer (1976:200) and Catlin (1844:238, plate 101) give similar descriptions of scalping. Although there is much in the Catlin account which is not supported by the osteological evidence (see Willey and Bass 1978:3-4), his illustration (Fig. 13) is of interest. Note the scalping on the left, where the scalper has approached the foe from the rear, placed a foot on the victim's neck and taken the scalp much as Adair describes. The descriptions and illustration of the procedure, while somewhat simplified, are consistent with the marks found on the Crow Creek skulls.

Blows to the head seem to have been a common way of dispatching or mutilating a foe according to the historic records. Bryant and Murch (1864:115, 219, 253, 363-364), Camp (1976:96), Coleson (1977:22), Coues (1897:260), Godfrey (1974:113), Luttig (1964:124), Marquis (1967:15), Palmer (1887:3), Paulding (1974:10-11), U.S. Army (1887:4), and Vaughn (1963:94) all mention head bashing. Whatever instrument was handy was used, but gun butts, clubs, hatchets and stone hammers are frequently mentioned in the accounts. Certainly the Crow Creek massacre victims were subjected to similar blows judging from the depressed fractures.

Removal of the nose is infrequently recorded. There are two direct references (Bryant and Murch 1864:222; U.S. Army 1887:4), and there is one other possible reference. The possible reference is by Luttig (1964:124) who saw the body of a fort worker who had "his Head Broken, the Brains scattered about[;] his nose and ears cut off,....." Admittedly this reference is ambiguous and might be edited otherwise to have a different meaning. The low

Figure 13. Catlin's (1844:238, plate 101) illustration of scalpings in progress.

frequency of cuts near the nasal apertures from Crow Creek and the few historic references to cut noses suggest that the mutilation was less common in prehistoric and historic times than some other mutilations.

In contrast to nose cutting, severing heads from the body seems to have been fairly common in Plains Indian warfare. It is mentioned in many historic accounts (Bryant and Murch 1864:133-134, Denig 1928-29:491, Fletcher and LaFlesche 1905-06:434, Grinnel 1892:254, Marquis 1967:15, Mooney 1895-96:260, Wagner 1973:237). It seems that most of the severed heads were left on the battlefield. For instance, David (1937:215) writes that a Mexican with a wagon train "had been caught, killed, and scalped by the Sioux, after which his head had been cut off and used for a football." Sometimes, however, the head was taken from the field. Thompson (Coues 1897:262) observed that "My beau-pere's head was severed from his body even with his shoulders,.... The enemy had ... taken away the skull of another man for a water dish;...." Perhaps some of the Crow Creek skulls were taken for similar uses. If removal from the Crow Creek Site occurred, then the minimum count of individuals based on temporals was less than its actual number. Based on specimens found in the bone bed, such trophy taking seems likely.

Thompson mentioning a skull being taken as a water dish is interesting. There are four possible bowls made from human skulls found at Crow Creek. Because of conflicting interest and a misunderstanding with one of the archaeologists, the "bowls" are not described as thoroughly as they might have been. Nevertheless some notes were made and photographs taken; this descriptions is based on those sources. All four skull caps consist of a partial frontal and parietals, and some may have included partial occipitals. All were found mixed with the rest of the bones in the fortification ditch, two of them coming from the same quarter-meter square. It is unclear if the bowls were made from the Crow Creek massacre victims, were kept formerly by the victims, or were included with the victims as trophies.

The bowls are described beginning with the most probable bowl and proceeding to the least likely. The edge of the most likely bowl (Box 107-Bag 2) appears to have been made by incising a groove, snapping the bones along the groove, then smoothing the broken edge. Based on the size and thickness of the bones, the skull is probably from a child. The other specimens are not as clear-cut as the first. The next most likely bowl (139-5, Skull 324) is from a male?, 25-35 years old. Rather than having the relatively complex sequence of grooving, snapping and smoothing of the first, this specimen appears to have been formed by well-placed fractures, most of them depressed rather than linear. Only a portion of the edge is smooth. The remaining two specimens (58-5 Individual A-B, Skull 69, adult and 58-5-C, subadult) are even less likely bowls. In both of these specimens, there are fractures around the vault, but no smoothing is apparent on the broken edge. It is possible that these skulls were merely mutilated by fracturing and never intended to function as bowls. However ambiguous these last two specimens are, at least the other two specimens seem to have been purposefully modified and may have functioned as bowls.

A couple of historic accounts mention throats being cut (Bryant and Murch 1864:206, 219, 394; Collins 1972:256). No Crow Creek specimens have been interpreted as having their throats cut. But because throat cutting and decapitation attempts might leave similar cuts on the anterior part of the cervical vertebrae, any throat cuttings at Crow Creek would have been interpreted as decapitation attempts. And it is possible, of course, that no cut marks would be left on the bone from throat cutting.

Evulsion, the removal of teeth, occurred in historic times. Luttig (1964:124) mentions that a fort worker, killed in the early 1800's, was mutilated, including having "his teeth Knocked out,...." There is another reference to evulsions on the Northwestern Plains (U.S. Army 1887:4).

Occasionally severed tongues are mentioned in the historic accounts (Bryant and Murch 1864:219, Vaughn 1963:94).

Although the head and neck appear to be the major focus of defacement, postcranial body parts were also mutilated. Our discussion of postcranial mutilation begins with the dismemberment of the limbs and limb parts, then proceeds to chewing by scavengers.

Some historic accounts mention that arms were severed from the body (Coues 1897:262, Fletcher and LaFlesche 1905-06, Grinnel 1892:254, Marquis 1967:15, Springer 1971:52, U.S. Army 1887:4). Fingers and hands seem to have been popular parts for dismemberment (Bryant and Murch 1864:206, 222, 253; Denig 1928-29: 491-492; Grinnel 1892:254; Marquis 1967:15; Palmer 1887:6; Spring 1969:93; U.S. Army 1887:4; Vaughn 1963:94). Hands and fingers were used as necklaces (Bourke 1887), as offerings (Boller 1959:151), and in games (Kelly 1871:143). Some of the finger and hand bones missing from Crow Creek may have served these purposes.

Some historic accounts mention legs being severed following battles (Bryant and Murch 1864:253, Camp 1976:122, Coues 1897: 262, Fletcher and LaFlesche 1905-06, Grinnel 1892:254, Marquis 1967:15). Feet and toes are also recorded as being taken (Coues

1897:262, Denig 1928-29, Grinnel 1892:254, Marquis 1967:15, Palmer 1887:6, Spring 1969:93, U.S. Army 1887:4, Vaughn 1963:94). No mention is made of what uses were made of the severed feet or toes. It is possible that some of the foot bones missing from the Crow Creek sample were taken as trophies.

Burning is occasionally mentioned in the historic literature (Bryant and Murch 1864:222, 403; Coleson 1977:22; Vaughn 1963:98). For the most part burning the bodies seems to have occurred only when fires happened to be burning at the time the person was killed or when fires were being set to destroy property. Fires do not appear to have been made specifically to mutilate the bodies. Swegle (in Zimmerman et al. 1981:182-186) comes to many of these same conclusions concerning the Crow Creek burnings.

Historic accounts commonly mention scavengers devouring human bodies (Boller 1966:141; Coleson 1977:22, 23, 55). A few days after a battle between two Indian groups, Alexander Henry (Coues 1897:264) walked over the field noting that wolves and crows "interred" many of the dead; they did their job so thoroughly and so little remained that "I gathered up the remaining bones of my belle-mere in a handkerchief." Few accounts are as graphic as Keim's (1870:143) description of the Washita battlefield a few days after the fight.

> As we moved closer to the immediate site of the village, our approach breaking upon the quiet surroundings of the scene of death, and alarmed from their sense of security and enjoyment, fled innumerable beasts and birds of prey. Suddenly lifting from the ground could be seen thousands of ravens and crows, disturbed in their carrion feast. The dense black mass, evidently gorged, rose heavily, and passing overhead, as if to take revenge for molestation, set up the greatest confusion of noises. The cowardly wolves started from their abundant repast on human flesh, reluctantly left the spot, and while slowly getting out of reach of danger often stopped to take a wishful look behind.

The same sort of scavenging must have taken place at Crow Creek. In addition to birds and wild animals, domestic dogs are also known to eat bodies (Catlin cited in Dunn 1963:187, Thompson 1916). The Crow Creek victims were doubtlessly exposed to scavenging by their own dogs.

Parenthetically it is worth speculating about the village dogs consuming their masters. Dogs were eaten by many Plains Indian groups (e.g., Brackenridge 1906, v. 6:114, Gilmore 1933) and some individuals apparently still do (R. Alex, personal communication). Given the likely consumption of dogs by the villagers, we have to wonder if, as the village dogs consumed their masters, any of them appreciated the irony of the act as much as the feast.

There are a number of mutilations listed in the historic accounts which were not found in the skeletal series. Their absence may be because they did not occur at Crow Creek, they did occur but were not observed, or they did occur but left no or at best ambiguous osteological indications. Whatever the case, the variety of these other historically chronicled mutilations are informative.

One historic reference (Palmer 1887:3) records that a man's whiskers were cut off. Assuming that the Crow Creek men had whiskers, if cuts were present, they might have been missed. It is also possible that the cut whiskers were part of a more general facial mutilation. Several references (Bryant and Murch 1864:206, Paulding 1974:11, U.S. Army 1887:4) mention cuts on the bones of the face. There are a number of Crow Creek specimens with cuts on the face. Skull 51 is cut on the left alveolar process of the mandible, Skull 116 is cut on the middle of the zygomaxillary suture, Skull 197 is cut on the right zygomatic, Box 107-Bag 5 is cut on the right maxilla, and 164-11 is cut on both maxillae and left zygomatic. Perhaps these cuts resulted from their faces being cut as mentioned in the historic accounts.

A few historic accounts record ears being cut from the head (Boller 1959:151, Bryant and Murch 1864:222, Palmer 1887:6, Paulding 1974:11, Springer 1971:52, U.S. Army 1887:6). While it is possible that these references actually record the ears being taken with the hair during scalping, it may be that severing ears is a distinct mutilation. If it is a distinct mutilation and did occur at Crow Creek, then cuts on the Crow Creek crania near the ear may have been misinterpreted as scalping marks rather than ear removal.

Many historic accounts mention disembowelings (Byrant and Murch 1864:206, 253; Camp 1976:248; Coleson 1977:23; Coues 1897:262; Custer 1962:255; Godfrey 1974:112-113; Marquis 1967:15; Paulding 1974:11; Roe 1927:10; Spring 1969:93; Vaughn 1963:94; U.S. Army 1887:4). The cuts and breaks associated with eviscerating were not specifically searched for during our investigation of the Crow Creek remains. It is unlikely that these mutilations would have been fortuitously found. The same is true of genital severing which is mentioned in some historic accounts (Coues 1897:262, Custer 1962:225, Denig 1928-29:124, Dorsey 1881:313, possibly Luttig 1964:124, U.S. Army 1887:4, Wagner 1973:237). Their marks are unlikely to have been left on bone; none were observed at Crow Creek.

Perforating corpses with arrows (Camp 1976:95, Coues 1897:262, Luttig 1964:124, Palmer 1887:3, U.S. Army 1887:4, Vaughn 1963:94), spears (U.S. Army 1887:4, Vaughn 1963:94), bullets (Camp 1976:223), and knives (Coleson 1977:22) are all cited in historic accounts. There were few projectile points associated with the Crow Creek bones and punctures left by points after the points were removed may have been easily overlooked.

The evidence from Crow Creek does indicate, however, that either the historic custom of perforating the body with projectiles was not practiced at Crow Creek or the projectiles fell out or were removed before interment.

Plains Indian cannibalism is mentioned in a few historic records. During her captivity by the Sioux, Coleson (1977:23) observed,

> they would sear the tenderest parts of the victim's body with lighted pine torches, tear out the entrails and pluck off the scalp. In some instances they cut of [f?] the breasts of women, roasted the flesh and compelled the survivors to partake of it.

It is noteworthy that it was the surviving Whites, according to this account, who were forced to cannibalize, not the Indians. In another account, Godfrey (1974:112) mentions a Sioux warrior claiming to have removed and eaten the heart and liver of Tom Custer, George Custer's brother, following the Battle of the Little Big Horn. It is difficult assessing the accuracy of either historic account, but if cannibalism did occur historically on the Plains, it seems to have been a relatively incidental part of mutilation following battles and would have left few osteological indications.

The osteological evidence for cannibalism is always ambiguous, wherever the material originates. Researchers who have dealt with this question in other regions (e.g., Brothwell 1961, Eddy 1966, Flinn et al. 1976, Hough 1903, Jacob 1972, Nickens 1975, Phelps and Burgess 1964, Robbins 1974, Trinkaus 1985, Turner and Morris 1970, Turner 1983) have used a variety of criteria to indicate the cannibalism of archaeological remains. These criteria include disarticulated, often commingled remains, sometimes scattered in middens. Disproportionately represented elements have been used to indicate butchering and transportation of selected body parts. The bones were almost always broken while still fresh. The brains were often exposed, and the limb bone shafts were missing their ends, sometimes with the marrow scoured and sometimes with the shafts longitudinally split in an attempt to remove the marrow. The bones were often burned and cut. These modifications have been compared with similar modifications to the bones of animals which presumably were consumed.

It should be noted, as most of these authors have, that there are explanations for these modifications and for these archaeological contexts other than cannibalism. Disarticulation, commingling and scattering may have been caused by scavenging, mortuary processing, mutilation, or post-burial disturbance, such as animal burrowing, human digging, or physical erosion. Disproportionate representation of elements may be from normal attritional processes, such as scavenging animals, rather than from selective butchering during cannibalism. Broken skulls may be caused by the fragility of the bones, mutilation, or production of skull bowls rather than attempts to gain access of the brain for consumption. Split diaphyses may be caused by pressures of any sort, not just human attempts to expose and consume bone marrow. Burned bone may be from purposeful cremation or incidental contact with fire, not from cooking alone. Cutting may be from mutilation, mortuary processing or pseudo-cutting produced by animal gnawing and chewing. Each of these characteristics of cannibalism has alternative explanations, but when all are taken together, especially emphasizing the archaeological context, support can be mustered for a few archaeological examples of cannibalism. Crow Creek is not one of these instances.

Many of the same osteological modifications and archaeological contexts used as evidence for cannibalism are present at Crow Creek. Many skulls were broken while fresh and some of the limb bones were missing their ends. A few Crow Creek elements were burned and some were cut, although the cuts were most frequent on the bones of the head and neck, not the postcranial elements. On the other hand, some modifications were infrequent or absent. There were few large longitudinal splinters and little burning, and no marrow scouring was found. The remains were partly disarticulated, and rather than being scattered, they were concentrated in one location. Although some cannibalism may have occurred at Crow Creek, there is no incontrovertible archaeological or osteological evidence that it happened. If cannibalism did indeed occur, it probably had only a minor influence on the mutilation, disarticulation, and distribution of the Crow Creek elements.

C. Summary

Many kinds of mutilations are represented on the bones of the Crow Creek villagers. Not only are there many kinds of mutilations, but some are present on virtually all individuals.

About 90 percent of the crania show evidence of scalping. This frequency is even more impressive when two possible healed scalpings and the fact that it is possible to scalp without leaving cuts are considered. The actual frequency of scalping may approach 100 percent. There seems to be no sex difference in the style or side of scalping among adults, but there are differences by age. In general the children are scalped higher on the skull vault than the adolescents or adults. A typical scalping consists of primary, circling cuts beginning in the midfrontal area and proceeding posteriorly; these cuts limit the amount of scalp taken. In addition to the primary cuts, there are secondary, scattered cuts within the area scribed by the primary cuts; these cuts aid skinning the scalp from the head. There are many variations from the typical scalping process, including where the circling cuts are located on the frontal, the presence of cuts on the occipital, and the association of primary cuts with some depressed fractures.

Depressed fractures are present in about 40 percent of the more complete skulls, usually located on the tops of the vaults. In most cases, one fracture is present, although as many as five are recorded. The shapes of the better preserved fractures are either round or ellipsoid.

Decapitation is indicated by cuts on the occipital and first two cervical vertebrae. About 25 percent of the individuals are mutilated in this way with the cuts concentrated on C-1 and on the anterior and right surfaces. It is possible that some of these cuts are from throat cutting rather than decapitation.

There are three facial mutilations which are noted with some frequency. A few--less than 5 percent--nasal apertures are cut, suggesting nose removal or face slashing. Evulsions are relatively common, present in about a quarter of the more complete jaws. And there is some evidence that tongues are severed by cutting through the underside of the jaw, the same way historic accounts indicate bison were butchered.

Postcranial cuts suggesting dismemberment are fairly infrequent, but those few cuts present are more common on elements from the right side than the left, like the decapitations. Other possible indications of purposeful dismemberment include snapping and splintering. From the most to least frequent, the snapped or splintered elements come from the toes, arms, fingers, ankles, feet, lower leg, and lower arm. It is certainly possible that snapping and splintering, rather than being purposefully done by the raiders, are indicative of animal scavenging.

Chewing is most frequent on cancellous bones which have projections and on the ends of long bones. The most likely scavengers responsible for the marks are wolves, coyotes and village dogs.

Burning is relatively light and infrequent at Crow Creek with those few burned elements being charred, not calcined. Parts of at least seven individuals are charred. The charred skulls appear to have been burned after scalping.

It is apparent from the above summary that mutilations and scavenging at Crow Creek are varied in kind and numerous, with the frequency of some kinds of mutilations approaching 100 percent. The effort to mutilate and disfigure the bodies was extensive.

The mutilation of the Crow Creek specimens is compared with the bones from the Crow Creek Village proper and Larson Village, and with mutilations described in historic accounts. Although the Crow Creek Village bones have few mutilations compared to those of the massacre victims, the sample size is small and little can be safely concluded from its examination.

Nearly all mutilations found at the prehistoric Crow Creek massacre are also present in the protohistoric Larson Village material, although generally less frequent. Absences of mutilations at Larson Village appear to be due either to Larson's small sample size or differing mutilation techniques. The low frequencies of mutilations at Larson Village appear to be caused by the inaccessibility of some bodies and perhaps the inclusion of some non-murdered individuals in the sample. Otherwise there seems to be continuity in mutilation patterns from the prehistoric to the protohistoric period.

The historic accounts of mutilation on the Northern Plains and surrounding areas are examined. The historic accounts mention all those mutilations found at Crow Creek and aid in understanding the mutilations which are not found on the Crow Creek bones. There are some recorded mutilations which are not found on the Crow Creek bones. These absences could be from misinterpreting the skeletal evidence or from a lack of resulting skeletal modifications. Examples of historic mutilations not found in the Crow Creek material include whisker and ear cutting, disemboweling, and perforation of corpses. But in general, it is apparent that mutilating the dying and recently dead did not originate during historic times, but stretches back through the protohistoric period and from there back at least into the fourteenth century. By the fourteenth century, as shown at Crow Creek, the general patterns are well-established.

Chapter 7
Crow Creek Stature

Growth and ultimate attainment of adult stature is produced by a combination of genetic and environmental influences and their interaction. Genetic influences have been demonstrated by twin studies (Shields 1962, Vandenburg 1962, Wilson 1976), resemblance of same-aged siblings (Garn et al. 1969, Garn and Rohmann 1966, Howells 1953, Mather and Jenks 1963, Tanner 1960:43-58), and parent-child correlations (Bielicki and Welon 1966, Howells 1966, Tanner et al. 1970, Tanner and Israelsohn 1963). Despite genetic influences, a myriad of environmental conditions affect stature.

These environmental influences affecting stature include nutrition (MacWilliam and Dean 1965, Graham 1968), disease (Prader et al. 1963), socio-economic level (Baird 1974, Clements and Pickett 1952, Gregor 1979, Thomson 1959), urbanization (Tanner and Eveleth 1976), possibly physical activity (cf. Eveleth and Tanner 1976:257-258), psychosocial stress (Friend and Bransby 1947, MacCarthy and Booth 1970, Widdowson 1951), and secular trend (Barett and Brown 1971, Charzewski and Bielicki 1978, Hagen et al. 1961, Takahashi 1966, Tobias 1972, Vlastovsky 1966). Clearly there are many variables which influence stature.

Change in sexual dimorphism--the proportional differences between the sexes--in modern populations has been explained in a variety of ways. Most authors (Bielicki and Charzewki 1977, Hiernaux 1968, Tobias 1972) attribute changes in dimorphism to environmental influences. Under ideal environmental circumstances, according to this explanation, both sexes attain their entire genetic potential for growth. But under harsh conditions, the males attain proportionately less of their potential growth than the females; consequently, the population's sexual dimorphism decreases. Other authors (Eveleth 1975,

Stini 1975) argue that genetic factors are more influential than environmental ones, while some (Gray and Wolfe 1980) argue that both environmental and genetic factors influence dimorphism. And yet others (Hall 1982) prefer behavioral explanations.

It is worthwhile considering these influences relative to Crow Creek size and dimorphism. Crow Creek femur length and dimorphism are compared with those of other, similar samples from the same region. Crow Creek stature is estimated to flesh-out this picture of the massacre victims.

A. Methods and Materials

Because skeletal stature is based on limb bone length and a formula, bone length is a more direct measure of size and not subject to formula assumptions and calculation errors. Of the limb bones, the femur is as accurate an indicator of stature as any other single long bone (Trotter 1970:77, table 28). An added benefit of using the femur is that it is one of the most sexually dimorphic of the limb bones (Black 1978, Dwight 1904-05, Pearson 1917-19) so sex can be determined with a high degree of accuracy. For these reasons, femur length is used to describe Crow Creek size and compare it with the other samples. Stature estimations are made only to present an approximation of the victims' heights during life.

Because there are size differences between sexes, the femora must be separated by sex before any descriptions or comparisons can be made. Innominate morphology is generally considered the most reliable part of the skeleton for visual sex determination (Phenice 1969, Kelley 1978). However, this area cannot be used in an analysis of the Crow Creek femora because few femora were articulated to innominates. To achieve adequately sexed samples, sex determination must be made from the femora alone. Univariate metric methods are frequently used (cf. Black 1978, Dwight 1904-05, Pearson 1917-19, Thieme 1957), but multivariate techniques are generally more reliable.

Multivariate sex estimation of postcranial remains has been used successfully on a variety of samples. Examples of multivariate femur sexing include Pons (1955), Thieme (1957), Thieme and Schull (1957), Hanihara (1958), Howells (1964), Giles (1970), and Kobyliansky et al. (1978). Most studies correctly sex 90 percent of the base samples.

Because of morphological variation among sex and ethnic groups, the more similar the sample which the discriminant functions are established are to the sample to be sexed, the more accurate the sex determinations will be. Consequently to estimate the sexes of the Crow Creek femora, it is best to calculate a discriminant function on similar, sexable femora. The adult left femora from the Larson Site (39WW2) near Mobridge, South Dakota, are used to establish a discriminant function. The Larson material has the advantages of being well-preserved, morphologically similar to Crow Creek, and sexed by innominate morphology.

In all cases the Larson Site femora employed in establishing the sex discriminant were sexed by innominate morphology. Phenice's (1969) method, the most accurate visual technique (Kelley 1978), was used whenever possible. When Phenice's method was not applicable, other, standard innominate characteristics were used, such as parturitional pitting (Stewart 1970, Houghton 1974, Ullrich 1975), sciatic notch (Bass 1971:159-161), and pubis length (Bass 1971:160). All sex determinations were made by Willey.

Femur length measurements were taken with an osteometric board and diameters with a sliding caliper. All measures of the Crow Creek femora were taken by Roger Williams, then a student at the University of South Dakota. Only left femora were used in this analysis. Willey took all measurements on the Larson material, as well as nearly all of the other comparative samples. The rest of the comparative samples are in Bass' file.

Femur measurements used to establish the sex discriminant are maximum length, bicondylar length, anterior-posterior and transverse midshaft diameters, and maximum head diameter. These measurements are defined below.

1. Maximum femur length. With either of the distal condyles against the osteometric board's fixed end, the proximal end is rocked in a circular motion against the movable end until maximum length is found (Bass 1971:168).

2. Bicondylar femur length. With both of the distal condyles against the osteometric board's fixed end, the proximal is moved up and down against the movable end to obtain the greatest bicondylar length (Bass 1971:168)

3. Maximum diameter of head. The greatest diameter is found by rotating the calipers any direction with both caliper arms on the proximal articular surface. Maximum diameter is usually found near the periphery of the articular surface (Bass 1971:168).

4. Anterior-posterior midshaft diameter. The midpoint on the shaft is located when maximum length is taken and marked with a pencil. Anterior-posterior diameter is taken from the linea aspera to the anterior surface while the caliper is held perpendicularly to the shaft's long axis. The posterior margins of the distal condyles are used to establish the anterior-posterior plane (Bass 1971:168).

5. Transverse midshaft diameter. It is measured in a similar way to anterior-posterior midshaft, but at right angles to anterior-posterior (Bass 1971:168).

Only those Larson specimens with all five measurements are used in establishing the sex discriminant; the Larson sample sizes are present in Table 48. The discriminant function

Table 48. Approximate dates, femur sample sizes, means, standard deviations, and dimorphism of Crow Creek and other sites.

Site	Approximate Date	Males			Females			Dimorphism
		N	Mean	S.D.	N	Mean	S.D.	
Crow Creek 39BF11	1325	44	442.0	23.2	41	407.5	15.5	8.12
Rygh 39CA4	1625	8	449.9	13.7	4	408.8	24.4	9.57
Mobridge 1 39WW1	1650	14	455.1	20.4	16	414.4	17.9	9.36
Mobridge 2 39WW1	1725	10	448.6	13.7	7	412.6	8.2	8.36
Larson 39WW2	1765	59	445.9	16.8	66	417.4	20.4	6.60
Leavenworth 39CO9	1817	29	450.5	22.1	25	423.1	17.4	6.27

subprogram in the SPSS program (Nie et al. 1975) is used to calculate the following formula using the two best discriminating measurements:

Discriminant score = (Femur head diameter x 0.4314251) +

(Femur anterior-posterior midshaft x 0.1518143) - 23.66658

Male $\bar{X}$ = 1.23477   Female $\bar{X}$ = -1.30336

Sectioning point = -0.034295

The portion of the Larson femora correctly classified is 90.0 percent. The formula is applied to all Crow Creek left femora which have the two measurements required for sex determination and maximum length.

Once sex is determined for each Crow Creek femur, femur length means and standard deviations are calculated (Table 48) using the CONDESCRIPTIVE routine SPSS (Nie et al. 1975). From the means, sexual dimorphism is calculated. Sexual dimorphism is defined as

$$\text{Sexual dimorphism} = \frac{\text{Male } \bar{X} - \text{Female } \bar{X}}{\left[\frac{\text{Male } \bar{X} + \text{Female } \bar{X}}{2}\right]} \times 100$$

The Crow Creek sexual dimorphism and femoral lengths by themselves mean relatively little. It is only through comparisons with other, similar samples that an understanding of their meaning can be achieved. Samples from five other sites are used in the comparison: namely, Leavenworth (39CO9), Larson (39WW2), Mobridge 1 (39WW1 F1), Mobridge 2 (39WW1 F2), and Rygh (39CA4). All samples are currently in the Bass Collection at the University of Tennessee, Knoxville. All samples appear to be Arikara or proto-Arikara based on cranial morphology (Jantz 1972, 1973), and it has been shown in Chapter 5 that Crow Creek appears also to be prehistoric Arikara based on craniometrics.

To test statistically the femora samples for differences, they are divided by sex and site. First a two-way analysis of variance (ANOVA) is performed using sex and site as independent variables and femur length as the dependent variable. The GLM routine in SAS (SAS Institute 1979) is employed to do the computations. The main purpose of this test is to see if differences in femur length exist between Crow Creek and other sites. To reveal which sites contained femora significantly different from others, ANOVA's are calculated separately for each sex using the same SAS program (SAS Institute 1979) used to calculate the over-all ANOVA for both sexes. Then these separate sex ANOVA's are used to inspect for pair-wise differences among the sites employing the Scheffe post hoc test.

Differences between Crow Creek femur lengths and those from other sites are also examined by linear and curvalinear regressions. The regressions are calculated by separating the sexes and using the estimated median date of site occupation as the independent variable and femur length as the dependent variable. Some dates (Table 48) are more accurate than others. The Leavenworth date, being historic, is accurate; the Crow Creek date is based on a C-14 date (Zimmerman et al. 1981). The other dates are approximations based on the presence or absence of Euroamerican trade goods. The dates for Mobridge 2 and Larson are probably fairly accurate, although, as noted before, the actual Larson date may be earlier than the one used here (cf. O'Shea 1984). The dates for Mobridge 1 and Rygh are rough approximations, based on the absence of Euroamerican trade goods. The regressions are calculated using the GLM routine in SAS (SAS Institute 1979). The main purpose of the regression analyses is to determine if a significant relationship exists between time and femur lengths.

To describe the appearance of the Crow Creek villagers, stature is estimated using Trotter's (1970:77, table 28) formula for Mongoloid males.

B. Results

The discriminant function calculated for sexing the Crow Creek femora produces reasonable results in terms of the number of each sex represented. There are 44 Crow Creek male (51.8 percent) and 41 female (48.2 percent) femora (Table 48). To test this distribution against that established using pubic morphology (see Chapter 4), a binomial Z-test is calculated. There is no statistically significant difference between the two sex distributions ($Z = 0.48782$, $F(Z) = 0.6879$, $P > 0.35$). Based on the information available, the Crow Creek femora sex estimations are accepted as reasonably accurate.

The femur descriptive statistics (Table 48) indicate that both the Crow Creek male and female means are smaller than any of the other like-sex samples. The Crow Creek standard deviations are approximately the same as those of at least some other sites.

To compare statistically the Crow Creek femora with those from the other sites, the ANOVA results are examined. The ANOVA of femur length by site and sex (Table 49) is highly significant ($F = 22.28$; $DF = 11, 311$; $P < 0.0001$), indicating that femur length varies by site or by sex. To determine which of the treatments--site or sex--contributes to the relationship, the partial F's are inspected (Table 49). The partials show that both sex and site are highly significant, although the interaction between site and sex is not. It has been

Table 49. Two-way ANOVA for Arikara femur length, site, and sex.

Source	DF	Sums of Squares	F-Value	Probability
Overall				
Model	11	88554.53	22.28	0.0001
Error	311	112378.42		
Total	322	200932.95		
Partial				
Site	5	5617.40	3.11	0.0095
Sex	1	47839.30	132.39	0.0001
Site*Sex	5	1643.08	0.91	0.4763

established from these tests that there is a statistically significant relationship among the variables, but it is yet to be established which sites have significantly different femora lengths from the other sites.

To reveal which sites' femora lengths are significantly different, ANOVA's of femur length by site are calculated for each sex separately. The ANOVA for the males is not significant by itself (Table 50), but the female ANOVA is. As a consequence of these results, only the female differences justify the subsequent Scheffe post hoc tests. Although the greatest female femur difference (Crow Creek vs. Leavenworth) approaches significance at the 0.05 level, neither this contrast nor any of the other pair-wise differences are significant. The explanation for the lack of significant pair-wise differences is probably the conservative nature of post hoc tests.

When the mean femur length for each site is plotted by sex against the sites' date of occupation, there appears to be a trend for earlier femora to be shorter and the later to be longer. Linear and curvalinear regression models are employed using femur length as the dependent variable and median occupation date as the independent variable. While the male regression (Fig. 14) has a positive slope (i.e., femur length increases with increasing time), the relationship is not statistically significant ($F = 2.72$; $DF = 1, 162$; $P < 0.10$). the female regression (Fig. 14) is also positive, but unlike the males' it is statistically significant ($F = 11.74$; $DF = 1, 157$; $P < 0.0008$). It can be stated confidently that the femur length of the Arikara females increases through time in our sample.

Interpreting these differences of femur length in terms of stature differences, the Crow Creek females average 160.18 cm (63 1/3 in) and the latest (Leavenworth) average 163.54

Table 50. One-way ANOVA's by sex for Arikara femur length and site.

Source	DF	Sums of Squares	F-Value	Probability
Males				
Model	5	2530.55	1.30	0.2656
Error	158	61479.81		
Total	163	64010.36		
Females				
Model	5	4521.29	2.72	0.0220
Error	153	50898.61		
Total	158	55419.90		

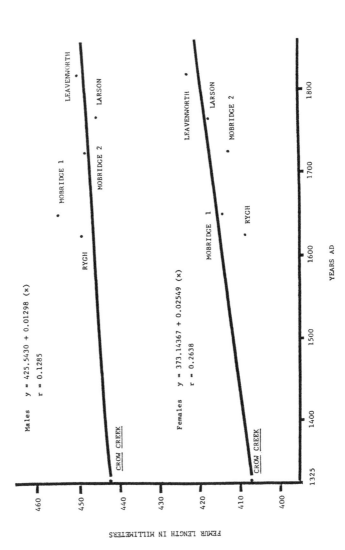

Figure 14. Relationship between time and Arikara femur length by sex.

cm (64 2/3 in). The average female stature increases 3.36 cm (1 1/3 in) during the 500 year period represented by the samples. On the other hand, the Crow Creek males average 167.6 cm (66 1/4 in) and at the latest site average 169.43 cm (67 in), an increase of only 1.83 cm (3/4 in).

Sexual dimorphism employs femur length, not the lengths' conversion into stature estimation. With the exception of Crow Creek, dimorphism consistently decreases through time (Table 48). The Crow Creek value falls near the mean of all the sites and is most similar to Mobridge 2.

C. Discussion

Since this study was completed, Zobeck (1983) has analyzed the limb bones from some of the same sites employed here. Because of the greater number of measurements he took, he omits the Crow Creek material, but adds samples from the three components at the Sully Site (39SL4) and generally has larger samples for the other sites which were used in both analyses. He finds no significant difference in femur length through time and no consistently decreasing sexual dimorphism. As Zobeck (1983:104, 107) points out, these differences may be caused by his inclusion of the Sully components, differences in measuring techniques, or differences caused by ontogenetic changes in samples which are demographically different. It should also be noted that Zobeck's samples exclude Crow Creek which had been reburied when he began collecting his data. The omission of Crow Creek is particularly important because both sexes in that sample are the smallest of any of the samples he used. Doubtlessly Crow Creek influences the statistical significance found here.

There are several points which should be made in this regard before proceeding with the rest of this discussion. Because Crow Creek is by far the earliest large sample from the Middle Missouri Region and because there are no other comparable early villager samples, Crow Creek stands as the lone skeletal sample representing the entire Initial Coalescent Variant. It is impossible at this time to compare Crow Creek with other samples from the variant.

So we must ask if Crow Creek is an aberrant outlier from the main course of Middle Missouri skeletal biology. If Crow Creek is skeletally aberrant, then using the sample as <u>the</u> Initial Coalescent representative leads to unfounded interpretations. Lacking not only other sizeable Initial Coalescent samples but any skeletal samples of note until 300 years later than Crow Creek makes many comparisons tenuous. This point is especially applicable to the analysis of femoral length. Crow Creek's early date and its possibly unusually short femur length may have produced results not representative of the Coalescent Tradition as a whole. Clearly the archaeological context and some of the skeletal studies (e.g., paleodemography) of Crow Creek suggest an aberrant situation.

For the purposes of the rest of this discussion, however, it is assumed explicitly that Crow Creek femur length, is representative of its variant and not an aberrant "blip" in the course of Middle Missouri skeletal biology. Additional skeletal samples will be needed before this assumption can be tested.

As noted in the introduction to this chapter, adult stature and sexual dimorphism result from the influences on subadult growth of the environment, genes, their interaction, and perhaps behavior. Although it is impossible to separate these influences in this study, it is heuristically useful to divide the discussion of stature into environmental, genetic and behavioral explanations. Sexual dimorphism is discussed following these discussions.

Environmental Explanations

It may be somewhat surprising, given the present results, that historic accounts chronicle hard lives for the Arikara, including nutritional problems, diseases, depopulation, and social disintegration. Some nutritional problems--like famines--were short-term, although apparently some people starved to death (Tabeau 1939:74, Maximilian 1906:335-336). Protein deficiency, on the other hand, may have been chronic (Trudeau 1914:458, cf. La Verendrye 1914). European diseases, particularly smallpox, ripped through the "virgin soil" populations, perhaps killing over 75 percent of the Arikara in a single epidemic (Lehmer and Jones 1968:91). Depopulation and social disintegration during the historic period are axiomatic.

There are no indications at Crow Creek that epidemic diseases, depopulation, or social disintegration were present before the raid. Nevertheless Crow Creek statures average less than any other site--even the highly stressed historic Leavenworth Site. If stature does reflect stress, then Crow Creek was even more stressed than the seemingly down-trodden historic Arikara.

In seeking explanations for these somewhat surprising differences, two related environmental effects are discussed here. The first part of the explanation interprets the Arikara stature change as one instance of a possibly world-wide process involving changing subsistence base and nutritional adequacy. The second part invokes changing climate as the fundamental mover, limiting available resources and producing differences in stature by the limited resources.

The stature increase found through time may represent a general process found elsewhere. In a classic article, Nickens (1976) finds that Mesoamerican stature decreases with the adoption of maize agriculture, bottoms some time later, then gradually increases. These changes he attributes largely to diet and diet-related pathology. Similar decreases in stature following the adoption of agriculture are found in many other parts of the world (cf. Cohen and Armelagos 1984). It may be that similar processes influenced Arikara stature. If the Arikara follow the general case, then we would expect stature reduction beginning about 900-1000 AD when agriculture becomes intensive and apparently begins to make a substantial contribution to subsistence (Lehmer 1971:32, 96; Wedel 1961:92). The shortest statures would be a little later. Then, as nutrition improves through time, stature increases.

To test the applicability of Nickens' model to the Arikara, morphologically similar samples are needed from the time periods preceding and following Crow Creek. Especially crucial are the hunter-gatherer samples. Unfortunately, the only large early sample is from the Hancock Site (25DK13), a St. Helena cemetery in northeast Nebraska. It is an ossuary thought to be slightly earlier or roughly contemporary with Crow Creek (Bass, unpublished notes). Bass kindly made his unpublished Hancock femur data available for this analysis.

The 23 Hancock male femur maximum lengths average 451.4 mm and the 23 females average 414.0 mm, both greater than those from Crow Creek and approximately the same as some of the later Arikara. These results may support the applicability of Nickens' model to the Arikara, but additional data are needed to test it fully. Before accepting Nickens' model as appropriate, we need to be certain that the suppression of stature at Crow Creek is due to changing subsistence patterns.

There is the additional concern that the observed low point (Crow Creek) may be too late to represent the same process that Nickens describes. In addition although the female statures are significantly different, it is inconsistent that the Arikara male differences are not statistically different.

There is another part to the environment explanation which may have influenced the short Crow Creek stature. That influence is the climate.

Lehmer (1970), using the paleoclimatic reconstruction of the Plains by Bryson and co-workers, notes that the Pacific I climatic episode began between 1200 and 1300 AD and ended in the mid 1400's, a period which includes the Crow Creek occupation. This episode is characterized by "Greater amounts of cool dry air, lowered temperatures and decreased precipitation" (Lehmer 1970:121). This climate would have had a marked affect on the natives. As Lehmer (1970:121) notes, these conditions

> would have been unfavorable for corn agriculture, and they may also have diminished the game supply by cutting back the grass cover available for pasturage. They also presumably inhibited tree growth through decreased precipitation and increased evaporative stress.

Following this episode, the climate became milder until the NeoBoreal, beginning about 1550, when the summers were cooler.

It is possible the climatic limitations of the Pacific I episode affected the Crow Creek inhabitants through chronic and seasonal nutritional deficiencies and the accompanying synergistic effects of disease. There is also the possibility that the intrusion of the Initial

Coalescent groups into the Middle Missouri Region, displacing the previously indigenous Middle Missouri Tradition, compounded an already critical situation. The additional people living in an area marginal for corn-growing during a period of climatic stress may have made worse an already major problem. Perhaps the cause of the Crow Creek massacre was the Middle Missouri Region's total human population approaching the region's carrying capacity during a stressful time. As represented by the adult Crow Creek femur length, increased disease pressure and under- and malnutrition may have triggered the tragedy at Crow Creek.

Warfare at a technological level like Crow Creek would have temporarily reduced the number of people in the area both by those outright killed by the raid and by dispersion of any Crow Creek survivors into other villages in other locations. Warfare also would have spaced hostile groups and presumably the interstices between the groups would have been exploited less, hence allowing their resources more time to recover between uses.

It should be noted, however, that the femoral length data from later sites do not conform to expectations based on Lehmer's climatic reconstruction. As summarized by Jantz and Owsley (1984a:16), Lehmer's reconstruction suggests that the Extended Coalescent (represented in our samples by Rygh and Mobridge 1) climate was variable, the Post Contact Coalescent (Mobridge 2 and Larson) was adequate or good, and the Disorganized Coalescent (Leavenworth) was poor. The adult femur length data do not support these reconstructions, with the "poor" Disorganized Coalescent sample being among the largest and the "adequate or good" Post Contact Coalescent samples being smaller. Parenthetically it should be noted that Jantz and Owsley (1984a) find no difference in femur growth of children during these later variants.

While some of the environmental reasonings make sense, there is another problem with using stress as the sole explanation. The major problem is that present-day studies show that stressed males are more stunted than similarly stressed females (Eveleth and Tanner 1976). But when change in femur length through time is examined, it is the females who become larger, not the males. This observation is inconsistent with our expectations.

While not the expected case, these data are not unique. Joerschke (1983:75-82) studied femur length through time in Tennessee. Using a longer period (about 5000 years) and a more marked contrast in subsistence (hunter-gatherers vs. agriculturalists) than those analyzed here, the results of the Tennessee data are similar to the present study: namely, there is a significant difference among female femora with the earlier ones being shorter, but there is no difference in the males. A similar trend is noted for the Lower Illinois Valley (Cook 1984). It is appropriate to examine other explanations besides the environment.

Genetic and Behavioral Explanations

Another inconsistency with the environmental stress explanation is that it assumes no genetic change occurred through time, or if there was change, it had no influence on femur length and stature.

At least the first part of this assumption is violated. There is convincing historic evidence that gene flow was occurring between the Arikara and other Indian groups as well as whites (e.g., Tabeau 1939:180-181, Brackenridge 1906:129-130, Bradbury 1904:140, Luttig 1964:81, Trudeau 1914:460-461). Additional evidence supporting the presence of gene flow comes from the changing Arikara cranial measurements, which Jantz (1973) believes demonstrates flow.

It is also likely that selection was occurring. One early trader (Trudeau 1914:459) mentions differential familiar survival from smallpox. Osteological support for selection comes from Jantz and Willey's (1983) study of cranial height changes.

It is possible that differential survival explains stature change. According to this explanation, the shorter individuals, for some unknown reason, were less fit than taller individuals. The shorter individuals tended to die at a younger age and have fewer offspring. The taller people, on the other hand, would have tended to live longer and have more offspring. Depending on how strong and constant this tendency was, the populations may have become taller fairly quickly. This hypothesis could be tested partially by separating the femur samples into younger and older adult groups divided by site and sex and by applying an ANOVA to the data. At the moment, that additional analysis is beyond the scope of this study. If this explanation is correct, it still does not explain why female size changed and male size did not. A possible explanation employs pelvic size. There is some evidence that the Arikara female pelvis through time became larger in dimensions which may have improved the probability of successful childbirth. These increasing pelvic measurements may be related to increasing femoral length, and this association may explain why only females change. This possibility should be examined further, but it is beyond the scope of this study.

In addition to gene flow and selection, it is also possible, although unlikely, that gene drift may have happened through group endogamy. This probability is somewhat feasible for the earlier sites, but highly unlikely for the later sites based on historic accounts.

A final explanation for increasing female size involves behavioral changes. According to this explanation, an agricultural life is less demanding on females than gathering, thus allowing the females to grow larger (Frayer 1980). To be applicable to the sample used here, we would have to assume that adaptation to an agricultural life was gradual and became progressively easier for women through time. Again, the historic accounts are instructive. Tabeau (1939:148-149) describes the Arikara women as nothing short of slaves who work very hard, and Brackenridge (1906:175) writes that they do all of the drudge work. Both of these observers describe the Arikara women at the Leavenworth Site, the site with the longest female femora in our samples. If the behavioral interpretation is correct, then the work load of earlier periods would have been even more rigorous--at least for the women--than the historic.

Sexual Dimorphism

The femur sexual dimorphism of Crow Creek (Table 48) is less than the other prehistoric sites (Rygh and Mobridge 1), greater than the historic and one of the protohistoric sites (Leavenworth and Larson, respectively), and most closely approximates a protohistoric site (Mobridge 2). It is noteworthy that, with the exception of Crow Creek, dimorphism consistently decreases through time, from the prehistoric through the protohistoric and into the historic.

If we had nothing but the decreasing sexual dimorphism before us, it would support the environmental explanation of sexual dimorphism: namely, decreasing dimorphism with increasing depopulation, social disintegration, and stress. However, additional information is present in the form of femur length, and as has been noted in the previous section, femur length is inconsistent with an environmental explanation. Rather than decreasing male femur length through time, as would have been expected, the male length is unchanged statistically while the female length becomes greater, thus changing the dimorphism. Dimorphism fits nicely the environmental explanation, but the femur length data do not.

There are problems specific to the dimorphism discussion which should be noted. Because the Crow Creek remains were mostly disarticulated and few reliably sexed innominates were associated with their femora, a discriminant function, it will be recalled, was developed to determine sex directly from the femora themselves. Using a discriminant function to determine sex which is based on size and using these results to assess differences in size between the sexes is circular reasoning. This problem is compounded by the fact that the "known" sex femora on which this discriminant function was calculated is really skeletal sex, not known biological sex. And skeletal sex is in part based on size. Finally, using a sectioning point, as a discriminant function does, artificially truncates the length distribution by sex at the sectioning point; this process probably decreases each sex's variance. As a consequence of these problems, the Crow Creek dimorphism results should be viewed with caution.

D. Summary

Generally it is agreed that adult stature and sexual dimorphism are influenced by the effect of environment, genetics and/or behavior on the growing individual. From a skeletal standpoint, femur length is the most accurate indicator of stature, so femora are used in this analysis of size. The Crow Creek femora are sexed using a discriminant function developed on similar archaeological material; the function seems to give reasonable results for Crow Creek.

The Crow Creek males and females are the shortest of the six samples examined from the Middle Missouri Region. While the male differences are not statistically significant, the females are. There is a trend for the earlier sites in both sexes to be shorter than the later ones. Although the male increase through time approaches significance, only the female differences are statistically significant. When the Crow Creek statures are estimated from femur lengths, both sexes are medium in height. The sexual dimorphism consistently decreases through time with the exception of Crow Creek. Crow Creek's dimorphism is intermediate when compared with the other samples, but has less dimorphism than might be expected for this early period. Because the femur length and dimorphism results are somewhat inconsistent with those expected in the environmental, genetic or behavioral explanations, a single cause is unlikely. A combination of these causes or other unknown causes may be involved.

This comparison of Crow Creek's size with other samples rests on shaky foundations. While Crow Creek's femoral lengths may be representative of those from the Initial Coalescent Variant, it is also possible that the sample is aberrant and not actually representative of the variant. Additional early villager skeletal samples are needed to better assess Crow Creek's representativeness.

Chapter 8
Interpretation

The previous chapters have presented either background information or data from specific information sources. Generally the chapters dealing with specific information sources are limited in their scope to those data and inferences from those data. To present a more unified summary, this chapter combines results and conclusions in a chronological sequence from all chapters. The interpretation begins with background information, then presents inferences about the major events of the raid, exposure period, burial, and recovery.

A. Background

About 1325 AD in central South Dakota, the Crow Creek Village was destroyed, hundreds of people murdered, and their bodies buried in the fortification ditch which circled the village. The village is large, the principal ditch enclosing nearly 18 acres. The principal ditch stretches 1250 feet from the high bluff overlooking the Missouri River flood plain to a lesser, but still imposing, bluff above Crow Creek. Along the ditch's course, there are 10 bastions. There are at least 50 lodge depressions from the Initial Coalescent component of the site. There are some indications that during this period the climate was cooler and drier than before or after the occupation.

The victims are from the Initial Coalescent component and appear most similar to the Arikara tribe. There were probably more than 800 people living in the village, and at least 486 people were killed and buried in the ditch. The people from Crow Creek, most notably the women, were shorter than later Arikara. Their height may have been caused by an inadequate diet and marginal health which in turn may have been caused by the harsher climate.

B. The Raid

Calling the raid "catastrophic" is an understatement. The raid ended the lives of at least 486 people. Many lodges were burned and the functions of the village as a social unit, a fortress, and a home ended.

Perhaps the most striking osteological evidence of the raid were the mutilations. There are a great variety of mutilations, some of which occur with high frequency. Mutilations included scalping, blows to the head, evulsions, decapitation, burning, and dismemberment. Some noses and tongues were severed. Scalping was the most frequent mutilation; about 90 percent showed indications of scalping. This high incidence is even more remarkable because it has been demonstrated elsewhere that scalping does not always leave marks on the bones. All ages and both sexes showed scalping. Depressed fractures were present on 40 percent of the more complete skulls, and there were as many as five depressions on some skulls. The outlines of the depressions were either round or ellipsoid, the ellipsoid fractures being present twice as frequently as the round ones. Indications of decapitation were present in about a quarter of the individuals and were concentrated on the first cervical vertebra. Many of these mutilations would have been sufficient to cause death. Surprisingly few projectile points were recovered during excavation, suggesting that few were used or they were removed or fell out before burial.

There is evidence that the violence which ended the lives of the Crow Creek victims was not a unique event. Two skulls appeared to be from people who survived scalpings which occurred months or years before the raid. A third skull had a massive healed depressed fracture in the frontal. These three people survived earlier traumas only to die in the massacre.

Most of the killing and mutilating must have happened in and near the village during cold weather. Some mutilated bones were found during the excavation of some of the lodges. It also seems likely that some people may have been slaughtered outside the village. And, if historic sources are any indication, some people probably eluded the raiders altogether. The slayings must have happened during cold weather because the seasonally ubiquitous flies and other warm weather insects were absent.

There is evidence that some portions of the Crow Creek population were not buried in the ditch. Young adult females and old adult males are under-represented among the massacre victims. Historic sources often mention raiders taking young women captive, and this is probably what happened to some of the young Crow Creek women. The explanation for the absence of the old men is unknown.

Although the raiders left their marks on the victims, the raiders themselves remain anonymous. Mutilation patterns seem to lack tribal distinctions, and there appears to be a regional mutilation tradition stretching at least from fourteenth century Crow Creek into the protohistoric period and probably into the historic period. No craniometrically aberrant skulls were found at Crow Creek. If skulls of the raiders were included with those of the victims, then they are morphologically identical to the victims. And if that is so, then the raiders, too, were Arikara. But it is possible that no raider skulls were included with the victims.

C. Exposure

The victims were left exposed above ground for some time before being buried. During their exposure, the bodies became a carrion feast. Wolves, coyotes, and village dogs are the most likely to have consumed the flesh, but other mammals and birds are reasonable culprits as well. These creatures must have been a major cause of disarticulating the bodies and losing the extremities.

Based on the amount of dismemberment, there were either many scavengers, much time, or both. There are too many variables and too little is known about decomposition to estimate accurately the length of exposure. It is likely that the remains were above ground for more than a few days but less than several months. A period of less than several weeks seems to be the most likely, although these estimations are highly speculative.

D. Burial

The exposed bodies were buried at the extreme northwest corner of the village in the fortification ditch, the ditch which was supposed to protect the villagers. The protector became their crypt.

The body parts and bones were picked up probably by returning villagers who had escaped the massacre or by otherwise affiliated people. Recovering all body parts was impeded at least in part by the burned, collapsed lodges. It is also possible that recovery was impeded by drifted snow. Recovery was even further impeded by the scattering by the raiders and the scavengers. Some parts, especially the hands and feet, may have been lost before the recovery effort, and it is possible that many small bones were overlooked by the buriers. Certainly, for one reason or another, bones were left in some of the lodges, as indicated by previous excavations.

The body parts were carried to the extreme northwest part of the site and piled deeply--at one place over 4 feet deep--in the ditch. There apparently was no systematic attempt to align the parts, although this effort may have been impossible given the conditions of the remains. Rather, the parts were piled against the north wall of the ditch, forming a cone against the wall and spilling away from the peak across the ditch to the south wall of the ditch and east and west along the main axis of the ditch. Surprisingly the element distribution showed no slope (north-south) differences in element distribution. What slight differences there are occur mainly along the east-west axis. Skulls seem to be what more frequent toward the northeast part of the deposit; hand and wrist bones are more frequent toward the southwest. No kin distinctions were made in the placement of skulls in the deposit, at least not along the main, east-west axis. But the faces and other body parts may have been beyond recognition by the time of the burial. Finally, after the bones were in place, they were covered with a thin layer of clay.

Above the principal bone bed and the clay covering was a thin, scattered layer of bones. The reason for this secondary deposit is unclear. The deposit could have been "leftovers" remaining from scavengers which dug into the primary deposit and hauled up parts to consume. An alternative explanation for the secondary deposit is that there was a second recovery of bones after the first was buried and these bones were placed in the ditch above the primary bone bed. It is unclear which of these explanations is correct.

It is likely that there are other bones at Crow Creek. It is almost certain that bones are still scattered in the village as demonstrated by the earlier excavations of some of the lodges. Certainly at least a few bones remain unexcavated in the primary bone deposit. It is also possible that there are additional large bone deposits. Because the village is 450 yards long and the excavated bone beds are at the extreme northwest corner of the village, it seems likely that there may be additional burial locations at more convenient locations.

E. Excavation and Reburial

Excavation of the remains began in 1954 and 1955 when Kivett and the Nebraska State Historical Society worked in the Crow Creek Village exposing several lodges and other features. The events which led to the presence of the scattered bones in their excavations and the burned lodges were unclear at that time. With the 1978 discovery of the bones in the fortification ditch, the nature and magnitude of the events became apparent.

By 1978 a headwardly eating gully had followed the end of the fortification ditch to the west end of the bone bed and exposed parts of several individuals. Before excavations were begun by the University of South Dakota crew, a portion of the bed was looted, the bones broken and strewn down the gully. These remains were recovered, and almost all the rest of the bone beds were excavated, but because of limited time and money, a few bones remained covered at the east end of the excavation.

The bones were studied at the University of South Dakota beginning in January 1979 and returned in May 1979 to the Crow Creek Sioux Reservation for reburial. Reburial occurred in August 1981 using one of the excavation pits dug in the 1950's by the Nebraska State Historical Society as the grave. There they rest today.

REFERENCES CITED

Adair, J.
1775   The History of the American Indian. London: Edward and Charles Dilly.

Alex, Robert
1978   Personal communication. Conversation, August 1978.

Administrative Rules of South Dakota
1986   Title 24 Department of Education and Cultural Affairs. Published by the South Dakota Code Commission.

Audubon, Maria R.
1897   Audubon and His Journals. New York: Scribner and Son.

Baird, Dugald
1974   The Epidemiology of Low Birth Weight: Changes in Incidence in Aberdeen, 1948-72. Journal of Biosocial Science 6:323-342.

Barrett, M.J., and T. Brown
1971   Increase in Average Height of Australian Aborigines. Medical Journal of Australia 2:1169-1172.

Bass, William M.
1964   The Variation in Physical Types of the Prehistoric Plains Indians. Plains Anthropologist Memoir 1.

1971   Human Osteology: A Laboratory and Field Manual of the Human Skeleton. Columbia: Missouri Archaeological Society Special Publications.

Bass, W.M., and H.E. Berryman
1976   Physical Analysis. In Fay Tolton and the Initial Middle Missouri Variant. W.R. Wood (ed.). Missouri Archaeological Society Research Series 13:29-31.

Berry. A.C., and R.J. Berry
1967   Epigenetic Variation in the Human Crania. Journal of Anatomy 101:361-379.

Bielicki, T., and Z. Welon
1966   Parent-Child Height Correlations at Ages 8-12 in Children from Wroclaw, Poland. Human Biology 38:167-174.

Bielicki, T., and J. Charzewski
1977   Sex Differences in the Magnitude of Statural Gains of Off-Spring over Parents. Human Biology 49:265-277.

Black, Thomas K.
    1978   A New Method of Assessing the Sex of Fragmentary Skeletal Remains: Femoral Shaft Circumference. American Journal of Physical Anthropology 48:227-232.

Boller, Henry A.
    1959   Among the Indians: Eight Years in the Far West, 1859-1866. Chicago: R.R. Donnelley and Sons.

    1966   Journal of a Trip to, and Residence in, the Indian Country. North Dakota History 33:106-219, 260-315.

Bourke, J.G.
    1887   The Medicine-Men of the Apache. Bureau of American Ethnology, Report 9:43-46.

Boyd, Robert K.
    1925   The Battle of Birch Coulee. Eau Claire: Herges Printing.

Brackenridge, H.M.
    1906   Journal of a Voyage up the Missouri River Performed in Eighteen Hundred and Eleven. In Early Western Travels. R.G. Thwaites (ed.). Cleveland: Clark. Vol. 6.

Bradbury, John
    1904   Travel in the Interior of America in the Years 1807, 1810, and 1811. In Early Western Travels. R.G. Thwaites (ed.). Cleveland: Clark. Vol. 5.

Brothwell, Don R.
    1961   Cannibalism in Early Britain. Antiquity 35:304-307.

Bryant, C.S., and A.B. Murch
    1864   A History of the Great Massacre by the Sioux Indians in Minnesota. Cincinnati: Rickey and Carroll Publishers.

Bumsted, M.P.
    1985   Past Human Behavior from Bone Chemical Analysis--Respects and Prospects. Journal of Human Evolution 14(5):539-551.

Butler, William B.
    1976   Human Skeletal Remains: Context. In Fay Tolton and the Initial Middle Missouri Variant. W.R. Wood (ed.). Missouri Archaeological Society Research Series 13:27-29.

Camp, Walter Mason
1976   Custer in '76. Provo: Brigham Young University Press.

Carpenter, James Culver
1976   A Comparative Study of Metric and Non-Metric Traits in a Series of Modern Crania. American Journal of Physical Anthropology 45:337-344.

Catlin, George
1844   Letters and Notes on the Manners, Customs, and Conditions of the North American Indians. London: G. Catlin.

Charzewski, J., and T. Bielicki
1978   Is the Secular Trend in Stature Associated with Relative Elongation of the Limbs? Homo 39:176-181.

Cheverud, J.M., J.E. Buikstra, and E. Twichell
1979   Relationship between Non-Metric Skeletal Traits and Cranial Size and Shape. American Journal of Physical Anthropology 50:191-198.

Clements, E.M.B., and K.G. Pickett
1952   Height of Scotsmen. British Medical Journal 1:1300.

Cohen, M.N., and G.J. Armelagos (editors)
1984   Paleopathology at the Origins of Agriculture. Orlando: Academic Press.

Coleson, Ann
1977   Miss Coleson's Narrative of Her Captivity among the Sioux Indians. New York: Garland Publishing.

Collins, Dennis
1972   The Indians' Last Fight or the Dull Knife Raid. New York: AMS Press.

Cook, Della Collins
1984   Subsistence and Health in the Lower Illinois Valley: Osteological Evidence. In Paleopathology at the Origins and Agriculture. M.N. Cohen and G.J. Armelagos (eds.). Pp. 235-269.

Corruccini, Robert S.
1976   The Interaction Between Nonmetric and Metric Cranial Variation. American Journal of Physical Anthropology 44:285-294.

Coues, Elliot (editor)
  1897   New Light on the Early History of the Greater Northwest: The Manuscript Journals of Alexander Henry and David Thompson. Minneapolis: Ross and Haines.

Crothers, G., P. Willey, M. Swegle, and B. Bradtmiller
  ms   Cribra Orbitalia in the Crow Creek Massacre and Arikara Skeletal Series. Manuscript in Willey's possession.

Custer, George A.
  1962   My Life on the Plains. New York: Citadel Press.

David, Robert Beebe
  1937   Finn Burnet, Frontiersman. Glendale: Clark.

Denig, E.T.
  1928- Indian Tribes of the Upper Missouri. Bureau of American Ethnology,
  1929   Report 46:375-628.

DeSmet, Pierre-Jean
  1904   Letters and Sketches: With a Narrative of a Year's Residence among the Indian Tribes of the Rocky Mountains. In Early Western Travels. R.G. Thwaites (ed.). Cleveland: Clark. Vol. 27.

Dorsey, J.O.
  1881   Omaha Sociology. Bureau of American Ethnology, Robert 3:35-62.

Dunn, Adrian R.
  1963   A History of Old Berthold. North Dakota History 30:155-240.

Dwight, Thomas
  1904- The Size of the Articular Surface of the Long Bones as Characteristic of Sex;
  1905   An Anthropological Study. American Journal of Physical Anthropology 4:19-31.

Eastman, Mary
  1849   Dahcotah; or, Life and Legends of the Sioux around Fort Snelling. New York: John Wiley.

Eddy, Frank W.
  1966   Prehistory in the Navajo Reservoir District, Northwestern New Mexico. Museum of New Mexico Paper in Anthropology 15.

Emerson, Thomas E.
1979   Personal communication. Conversation, January 1979.

Eveleth, Phyllis B.
1975   Differences Between Ethnic Groups in Sex Dimorphism of Adult Height. Annals of Human Biology 2:35-39.

Eveleth, P.B., and J.M. Tanner
1976   Worldwide Variation in Human Growth. Cambridge: Cambridge University Press.

Ewers, John C.
1967   The Blackfeet. Norman: University of Oklahoma Press.

Fletcher, A.C., and F. LaFlesche
1905-   The Omaha Tribe. Bureau of American Ethnology, Annual Report 27:15-
1906   672.

Flinn, L., C.G. Turner, and A. Brew
1976   Additional Evidence for Cannibalism in the Southwest: The Case of LA 4528. American Antiquity 41:308-318.

Frayer, David W.
1980   Sexual Dimorphism and Cultural Evolution in the Late Pleistocene and Holocene of Europe. Journal of Human Evolution 9:399-415.

Friend, G.E., and E.R. Bransby
1947   Physique and Growth of Schoolboys. The Lancet 253:677-681.

Garn, S.M., K.P. Hertzog, and C.G. Rohmann
1969   Evidence for X-Linkage of Tibial Length and Body Length. American Journal of Physical Anthropology 31:187-190.

Garn, S.M., and C.G. Rohmann
1966   Interaction of Nutrition and Genetics in the Timing of Growth and Development. Pediatric Clinics of North America 13:353-380.

Gilbert, B.M., and W.M. Bass
1967   Seasonal Dating of Burials from the Presence of Fly Pupae. American Antiquity 32:534-535.

Gilbert, B.M., and T.W. McKern
1973 A Method for Aging the Female Os Pubis. American Journal of Physical Anthropology 38:31-38.

Giles, Eugene
1970 Discriminant Function Sexing of the Human Skeleton. In Personal Identification in Mass Disasters. T.D. Stewart (ed.). Pp. 99-109.

Gilmore, Melvin R.
1933 The Arikara Method of Preparing a Dog for a Feast. Papers of the Michigan Academy of Science, Arts, and Letters 19:37-38.

Godfrey, Edward S.
1974 The Two Battles of the Little Bighorn. New York: Liveright.

Graham, G.G.
1968 The Later Growth of Malnourished Infants; Effects of Age, Severity, and Subsequent Diet. In Calorie Deficiencies and Protein Deficiencies. R.A. McCance and E.M. Widdowson (eds.). Pp. 301-316.

Gray, J.P., and L. Wolfe
1980 Height and Sexual Dimorphism of Stature among Human Societies. American Journal of Physical Anthropology 53:441-456.

Gregg, J.B.
1982 Additional Information Regarding the Health of the Crow Creek Villagers. South Dakota Archaeology 6:69-82.

Gregg, J.B., and P.S. Gregg
1979 The Post-Mortem on Crow Creek. Paleopathology Newsletter 27:4-8.

1987 Dry Bones: Dakota Territory Reflected. Sioux Falls: Sioux Printing Company.

Gregg, J.B., and L.J. Zimmerman
1986 Malnutrition in Fourteenth-Century South Dakota: Osteopathological Manifestations. North American Archaeologist 7(3):191-214.

Gregg, J.B., L. Zimmerman, S. Clifford, and P.S. Gregg
1981 Craniofacial Anomalies in the Upper Missouri River Basin over a Millennium: Archaeological and Clinical Evidence. Cleft Palate Journal 18:210-222.

Gregor, Thomas
1979   Short People. Natural History 88:14-23.

Grewal, M.S.
1962   The Rate of Genetic Divergence of Sublines in the C57BL Strain of Mice. Genetic Research 3:226-237.

Grinnel, George Bird
1892   Blackfoot Lodge Tales: The Story of a Prairie People. New York: Scribner's Sons.

Hagen, W., G. Paschlau, and R. Paschlau
1961   Wachstrum und Gestalt. Stuttgart: George Thieme.

Hall, R.L.
1982   Units of Analysis. In Sexual Dimorphism in Homo sapiens: A Question of Size. R.L. Hall (ed.). New York: Praeger Publishers.

Hamperl, H.
1967   The Osteological Consequences of Scalping. In Diseases in Antiquity. D.R. Brothwell and A.T. Sandison (eds.). Pp. 630-634.

Hamperl, H., and W.S. Laughlin
1959   The Osteological Consequences of Scalping. Human Biology 31:80-89.

Hanihara, K.
1958   Sexual Diagnosis of Japanese Long Bones by Means of Discriminant Function. Journal of the Anthropological Society of Nippon 66:187-196.

Haug, J.
1990   New Law Protects Burials. Newsletter of the South Dakota Archaeology Society 20(1):4-5.

Hiernaux, J.
1968   Variabilite du Dimorphisme Sexuel de la Stature en Afrique Subsaharienne et en Europe. In Anthropologie und Humangenetik. K. Saller (ed.). Pp. 42-50.

Hough, Walter
1903   Archaeological Fieldwork in Northeastern Arizona: The Museum-Gates Expedition of 1901. U.S. National Museum Annual Report for 1901:279-358.

Houghton, Philip
    1974   The Relationship of the Pre-Auricular Groove of the Ilium to Pregnancy. American Journal of Physical Anthropology 41:381-390.

Howells, W.W.
    1953   Correlations of Brothers in Factor Scores. American Journal of Physical Anthropology 11:121-140.

    1964   Determination du Sexe du Bassin par Fonction Discriminante: Etude de Materiel du Docteur Gaillard. Bulletins et Memoires de la Societe d'Anthropologie de Paris 7:95-105.

    1966   Variability in Family Line vs. Population Variability. Annals of the New York Academy of Sciences 134:624-631.

Jacob T.
    1972   The Problem of Head Hunting and Brain-Eatting among Pleistocene Men in Indonesia. Archaeology and Physical Anthropology in Oceania 7:81-91.

Jaffe, A.J.
    1982   Personal communication. Letter dated March 29, 1982.

Jantz, Richard L.
    1970   Change and Variation in Skeletal Populations of Arikara Indians. Ph.D. dissertation, University of Kansas.

    1972   Cranial Variation and Microevolution in Arikara Skeletal Populations. Plains Anthropologist 17:20-35.

    1973   Microevolutionary Change in Arikara Crania: A Multivariate Analysis. American Journal of Physical Anthropology 38:15-26.

    1974   The Redbird Focus: Cranial Evidence in Tribal Identification. Plains Anthropologist 19:5-13.

    1976   Human Skeletal Remains: Discriminant Function Analysis. In Fay Tolton and the Initial Middle Missouri Variant. W.R. Wood (ed.). Missouri Archaeological Society Research Series 13:31-33.

    1977   Craniometric Relationships of Plains Populations: Historical and Evolutionary Implications. Plains Anthropologist Memoir 13:162-176.

    1982   Personal communication. Conversation, April 1982.

Jantz, R.L., and D.W. Owsley
1984a   Long Bone Growth Variation among Arikara Skeletal Populations. American Journal of Physical Anthropology 63:13-20.

1984b   Temporal Changes in Limb Proportionality among Skeletal Samples of Arikara Indians. Annals of Human Biology 11(2):157-163.

1985   Patterns of Infant and Early Childhood Mortality in Arikara Skeletal Populations. In Status, Structure and Statification: Current Archaeological Reconstructions. M. Thompson and M.T. Garcia, and F.J. Kense (eds.). Proceedings of the 16th Annual Conference of the Archaeological Association of the University of Calgary. Pp. 209-211.

Jantz, R.L., D.W. Owsley, and P.Willey
1978   Craniometric Relationships of the Central Plains Population. In The Central Plains Tradition: Internal Development and External Relationships. D.J. Blakelee (ed.). Office of the Iowa State Archaeologist Report 11:144-156.

Jantz, R.L., and P. Willey
1983   Temporal and Geographic Patterning of Relative Head Height in the Central Plains and Middle Missouri Areas. Plains Anthropologist 28:59-67.

Joerschke, Bonnie C.
1983   The Demography, Long Bone Growth, and Pathology of a Middle Archaic Skeletal Population from Middle Tennessee: The Anderson Site (40WM9). M.A. thesis, University of Tennessee, Knoxville.

Keim, de B. Randolph
1870   Sheridan's Troopers on the Borders: A Winter Campaign on the Plains. Philadelphia: Claxton, Remsen, and Haffelfinger.

Kelley, Marc A.
1978   Phenice's Visual Sexing Technique for the Os Pubis: A Critique. American Journal of Physical Anthropology 48:121-122.

Kelly, Fanny
1871   Narrative of My Captivity among the Sioux Indians. Cincinnati: Wilstach, Baldwin, and Company.

Key, Patrick J.
1983   Craniometric Relationships among Plains Indians: Culture-Historical and Evolutionary Implications. Department of Anthropology Reports of Investigations, University of Tennessee 34.

Key, P.J., and R.L. Jantz
    1981   A Multivariate Analysis of Temporal Change in Arikara Craniometrics: A Methodology 55:247-259.

    1990   Statistical Assessment of Population Variability: A Methodological Approach. American Journal of Physical Anthropology 82(1):53-59.

Kivett, M.F., and R.E. Jensen
    1976   Archaeological Investigations at the Crow Creek Site (39BF11). Nebraska State Historical Society Publications in Anthropology 7.

Kobyliansky, E., B. Arensburg, and Y. Rak
    1978   Sexing Bedouin Skeletons from Israel. Zeitschrift fur Morphologie und Anthropologie 69:205-208.

Langdon, S.P., P. Willey, P.H. Moore-Jansen, R.L. Jantz, L. Meadows, and R.W. Cummins
    1989   Human Skeletons from the South Dakota Archaeological Research Center. Report for the State of South Dakota and the South Dakota Archaeological Research Center, Contract no. 89C-061.

Larimer, Sarah L.
    1976   The Capture and Escape; or, Life Among the Sioux. New York: Garland Publishing.

La Verendrye, Le Chevalier de
    1914   Journal of La Verendrye, 1738-43. South Dakota Historical Collections 7:323-358.

Lehmer, Donald J.
    1970   Climate and Culture History in the Middle Missouri Valley. In Pleistocene and Recent Environments in the Central Great Plains. W. Dort and J.K. Jones (eds.). Pp. 117-129.

    1971   Introduction to Middle Missouri Archaeology. National Park Service Anthropological Papers 1.

Lehmer, D.J., and D.T. Jones
    1986   Arikara Archaeology: The Bad River Phase. Smithsonian Institution River Basin Surveys, Publications in Salvage Archaeology 7.

Loveland, C.J., J.B. Gregg, and W.M. Bass
    1984   Osteochondritis Dissecans from the Great Plains on North America. Plains Anthropologist 29(105):239-246.

Lowie, Robert H.
1935   The Crow Indians. New York: Farrar and Rhinehart.

Luttig, John C.
1964   Journal of a Fur-Trading Expedition on the Upper Missouri, 1812-1813. New York: Argosy-Antiquarian.

MacCarthy, D., and E.M. Booth
1970   Parental Rejection and Stunting of Growth. Journal of Psychosomatic Research 14:297-304.

MacWilliam, K.M., and R.F.A. Dean
1965   The Growth of Malnourished Children after Hospital Treatment. East African Medical Journal 42:297-304.

McKern, T.W., and T.D. Stewart
1957   Skeletal Age Changes in Young American Males: Analyzed from the Standpoint of Age Identification. Quartermaster Research and Development Command Technical Report EP-45. Natick, Massachusetts.

Marquis, Thomas B.
1967   Custer on the Little Big Horn. Lodi: Endkian Publishing.

Mather, K., and J.L. Jenks
1963   Correlations Between Relatives Arising from Sex-Linked Genes. Nature 198:314-315.

Maximilian, Alexander Phillip
1906   Travels in the Interior of North America. In Early Western Travels. R.G. Thwaites (ed.). Cleveland: Clark. Vols. 22, 23, 24.

Merchant, V.L., and D.H. Ubelaker
1977   Skeletal Growth of the Protohistoric Arikara. American Journal of Physical Anthropology 46:61-72.

Miller, George J.
1975   A Study of Cuts, Grooves, and Other Marks on Recent and Fossil Bone: II Weathering Cracks, Fractures, Splinters, and Other Similar Natural Phenomena. In Lithic Technology: Making and Using Stone Tools. Earl Swanton (ed.). Pp. 211-226.

Mooney, James
1895- Calendar History of the Kiowa. Bureau of American Ethnology, Annual
1896   Report 17:141-446.

Moorrees, C.F.A., E.A. Fanning, and E.E. Hunt
1963a Age Variation of Formation Stages of Ten Permanent Teeth. Journal of Dental Research 42:1490-1502.

1963b Formation and Resorption of Three Deciduous Teeth in Children. American Journal of Physical Anthropology 21:205-213.

Nickens, Paul R.
1975   Prehistoric Cannibalism in the Mancos Canyon, Southwestern Colorado. The Kiva 4:283-293.

1976   Stature Reduction as an Adaptive Response to Food Production. Journal of Archaeological Science 3:31-41.

Nie, N.H., C.H. Hull, J.G. Jenkins, K. Steinbrenner, and D.H. Bent
1975   Statistical Package for the Social Sciences. New York: McGraw-Hill.

O'Shea, John
1980   Personal communication. Letter dated December 2, 1980.

1984   Mortuary Variability: An Archaeological Investigation. Orlando: Academic Press.

Owsley, Douglas W.
1975   A Demographic Analysis of Skeletons from the Larson Site (39WW2), Walworth County, South Dakota. M.A. Thesis, University of Tennessee, Knoxville.

1978   Personal communication. Conversation, October 1978.

1981   Mobridge Site Cemeteries: Controversy Concerning the Location of the Over and Stirling Burials. Memoir of the Plains Anthropologist 17:43-56.

1985   Postcontact Period Nutritional Status and Cortical Bone Thickness of South Dakota Indians. In Status, Structure, and Stratification: Current Archaeological Reconstructions. M. Thompson, M.T. Garcia, and F.J. Kerse (eds.). Proceedings of the 16th Annual Conference of the Archaeological Association of the University of Calgary. Pp. 209-213.

Owsley, Douglas W.
1988   Osteological Evidence for Scalping in Coalescent Tradition Populations of the Northern Plains. Abstract published in Program and Abstracts of the 46th Annual Plains Conference.

Owsley, D.W., and W.M. Bass
1979   A Demographic Analysis of Skeletons from the Larson Site (39WW2), Walworth County, South Dakota: Vital Statistics. American Journal of Physical Anthropology 51:145-154.

Owsley, D.W., S.M. Bennett, and R.L. Jantz
1982   Intercemetery Morphological Variation in Arikara Crania from the Mobridge Site (39WW1). American Journal of Physical Anthropology 58:179-185.

Owsley, D.W., H.E. Berryman, and W.M. Bass
1977   Demographic and Osteological Evidence for Warfare at the Larson Site, South Dakota. Plains Anthropologist Memoir 13:119-131.

Owsley, D.W., and C.H. Hawkinson
1981   Infant Prematurity and Small-for-Gestational-Age Infants as a Measure of Disease and Nutritional Stress in Arikara Populations. Abstract of presented paper, American Journal of Physical Anthropology 54:260.

Owsley, D.W., and R.L. Jantz
1978   Intracemetery Morphological Variation in Arikara Crania from the Sully Site (39SL4), Sully County, South Dakota. Plains Anthropologist 23:139-147.

1985   Long Bone Lengths and Gestational Age Distributions of Post-Contact Period Arikara Indian Perinatal Infant Skeletons. American Journal of Physical Anthropology 68:321-328.

Owsley, D.W., C.E. Orser, R. Montgomery, and C.C. Holland
1985   An Archaeological and Physical Anthropological Study of the First Cemetery in New Orleans. Report to the Louisiana Division of Archaeology, Office of Cultural Development, Department of Culture, Recreation and Tourism, Baton Rouge.

Palkovich, Ann Marie
1978   A Model of Mortality and Its Application to Paleodemography. Ph.D. dissertation, Northwestern University.

Palmer, H.E.
1887   The Powder River Indian Expedition. Omaha: Republican Company.

Paulding, Holmes O.
1974   Surgeon's Diary: With the Custer Relief Column. Washington: South Capital Press.

Pearson, Karl
1917-   A Study of the Long Bones of the English Skeleton I: The Femur.
1919   Draper's Company Research Memoirs, Biometric Series X, Chapters 1-4.

Phelps, David S., and Rebekah Burgess
1964   A Possible Case of Cannibalism in the Early Woodland Period of East Georgia. American Antiquity 30:199-202.

Phenice, Terrell W.
1969   A Newly Developed Visual Method of Sexing the Os Pubis. American Journal of Physical Anthropology 30:297-302.

Pons, J.
1955   The Sexual Diagnosis of Isolated Bones of the Skeleton. Human Biology 27:12-21.

Prader, A., J.M. Tanner, and G.A. von Harnack
1963   Catch-Up Growth Following Illness or Starvation. Journal of Pediatrics 62:647.

Puskarich, Cheryl Lee
1984   Metric Variation in the Arikara Pelvis. Ph.D. dissertation, University of Tennessee, Knoxville.

Roberts, Ricky L.
1977   Population Estimates. In The Talking Crow Site: A Multi-Component Earthlodge Village in the Big Bend Region, South Dakota. Carlyle S. Smith (ed.). University of Kansas Publications in Anthropology 9:167-176.

Robbins, Louise M.
1974   Prehistoric People of the Mammoth Cave Area. In Archeology of the Mammoth Cave Area. Patty Jo Watson (ed.). Chapter 19, pp. 137-162.

Roe, Charles Francis
1927   Custer's Last Battle. New York: Robert Bruce.

Rose, J.C., M.K. Marks, M. Kay, and E.B. Riddick
1984   Analysis of Human Osteological Remains from Multi-County Areas, South Dakota. Report to the Omaha District Office of the U.S. Army Corps of Engineers under Contract no. DACW45-83-M-2506.

SAS Institute
1979   SAS User's Guide. Raleigh: SAS Institute.

Scott, D.D., R.A. Fox, M.A. Connor, and D. Harmon
1989   Archaeological Insights into the Custer Battle: An Assessment of the 1984 Field Season. Norman: University of Oklahoma Press.

Shermis, Stewart
1982-   Domestic Violence in Two Skeletal Populations. Ossa 9-11:143-151.
1984

Shields, J.
1962   Monozygotic Twins. London: Oxford University Press.

Smith, Marion W.
1938   The War Complex of the Plains Indians. American Philosophical Society Proceedings 78:425-464.

Snyder, L.M., and P. Willey
1989   Canid Modifications of Human Skeletal Remains: A Comparison of Archaeological Materials from Crow Creek, Modern Forensic Cases, and a Controlled Non-Human Sample. Paper presented to the Society for American Archaeology, April 1989, Atlanta, Georgia.

Spring, Agnes Wright
1969   Caspar Collins: The Life and Exploits of an Indian Fighter of the Sixties. Lincoln: University of Nebraska Press.

Springer, Charles H.
1971   Soldiering in Sioux Country: 1865. San Diego: Frontier Heritage Press.

Stewart, T.D.
1970   Identification of the Scars of Parturition in the Skeletal Remains of Females. In Personal Identification in Mass Disasters. T.D. Stewart (ed.). Pp. 127-135.

Stini, W.A.
1975   Ecology and Human Adaptation. Dubuque: W.C. Brown.

Suchey, Judy Myers
   1979   Problems in the Aging of Females Using the Os pubis. American Journal of Physical Anthropology 51:467-470.

Symes, Steven A.
   1983   Harris Lines as Indicators of Stress: An Analysis of Tibiae from the Crow Creek Massacre Victims. M.A. thesis, University of Tennessee, Knoxville.

Tabeau, P.A. (Annie Heloise Abel, ed.)
   1939   Tabeau's Narrative of Loisel's Expedition to the Upper Missouri. Norman: University of Oklahoma Press.

Takahashi, Eiji
   1966   Growth and Environmental Factors in Japan. Human Biology 38:112-130.

Tanner, J.M.
   1960   Genetics of Human Growth. In Human Growth. T.M. Tanner (ed.). Pp. 43-58.

Tanner, J.M., and P.B. Eveleth
   1976   Urbanisation and Growth. In Man in Urban Environments. G.A. Harrison and J.B. Gibson (eds.). Pp. 144-166.

Tanner, J.M., H. Goldstein, and R.H. Whitehouse
   1970   Standards for Children's Height at Ages 2-9 Years Allowing for Height of Parents. Archives of Disease in Childhood 45:755-762.

Tanner, J.M. and W.J. Israelsohn
   1963   Parent-Child Correlations for Body Measurements of Children between Ages One Month and Seven Years. Annals of Human Genetics 26:245-259.

Thieme, F.P.
   1957   Sex in Negro Skeletons. Journal of Forensic Medicine 4:72-81.

Thieme, F.P., and W.J. Schull
   1957   Sex Determination from the Skeleton. Human Biology 29:242-273.

Thomas, David Hurst
   1976   Figuring Anthropology. New York: Holt, Rinehart and Winston.

Thompson, David
   1916   David Thompson's Narrative of His Expeditions in Western America, 1784-1812. Toronto: Champlain Society.

Thomson, A.M.
1959   Maternal Stature and Reproductive Efficiency. Eugenics Review 51:157-162.

Tobias, P.V.
1972   Growth and Stature in Southern African Populations. In Human Biology of Environmental Change. D.J.M. Vorster (ed.). Pp. 96-104.

Todd, T. Wingate
1921   Age Changes in the Pubic Bone. II. The Pubis of the Male Negro-White Hybrid. III. The Pubis of the White Female. IV. The Pubis of the Negro-White Hybrid. American Journal of Physical Anthropology 4:1-70.

Trinkaus, Eric
1985   Cannibalism and Burial at Krapina. Journal of Human Evolution 14:203-216.

Trotter, Mildred
1970   Estimation of Stature from Intact Long Limb Bones. In Personal Identification in Mass Disasters. T.D. Stewart (ed.). Pp. 71-84.

Trudeau, Jean Baptiste
1914   Trudeau's Journal. South Dakota Historical Collections 7:403-474.

Turner, C.G.
1983   Taphonomic Reconstructions of Human Violence and Cannibalism Based on Mass Burials in the American Southwest. In Carnivores, Human Scavengers and Predators: A Question of Bone Technology. G.M. LeMoine and A.S. MacEachern (eds.). Proceedings of the 15th Annual Conference (Chacmool) of the Archaeology Association, University of Calgary. Pp. 219-240.

Turner, C.G., and N.T. Morris
1970   A Massacre at Hopi. American Antiquity 35:320-331.

Ubelaker, D.H., and R.L. Jantz
1979   Plains Caddoan Relationships: The View from Craniometry and Mortuary Analysis. Nebraska History 60:249-259.

Ubelaker, D.H., and P. Willey
1978   Complexity in Arikara Mortuary Practice. Plains Anthropologist 23:69-74.

Ullrich, Herbert
    1975   Estimation of Fertility by Means of Pregnancy and Childbirth Alterations at the Pubis, the Ilium, and the Sacrum. Ossa 2:23-39.

U.S. Army, Department of the Platte
    1887   Letter from the Secretary of War transmitting, in response to the resolution of February 11, 1887, report of Col. Carrington on the massacre near Fort Philip Kearney. Senate Executive Document 49th Congress, 2nd Session, no. 97.

Utermohle, C.J., and S.L. Zegura
    1982   Intra- and Interobserver Error in Craniometry: A Cautionary Tale. American Journal of Physical Anthropology 57:303-310.

Vandenberg, S.G.
    1962   How Stable Are Heritability Estimates? A Comparison of Heritability Estimates from Six Anthropometric Studies. American Journal of Physical Anthropology 20:331-338.

Vaughn, J.W.
    1963   The Battle of Platte Bridge. Norman: University of Oklahoma Press.

Vlastovsky, V.G.
    1966   The Secular Trend in the Growth and Development of Children and Young Persons in the Soviet Union. Human Biology 38:219-230.

Wagner, Glendolin Damon
    1973   Old Neutriment. New York: Sol Lewis.

Wedel, Waldo R.
    1961   Prehistoric Man on the Great Plains. Norman: University of Oklahoma Press.

Weiss, Kenneth M.
    1973   Demographic Models for Anthropology. Society for American Archaeology Memoirs 27.

Wheat, Joe Ben
    1972   The Olsen-Chubbuck Site: A Paleo-Indian Bison Kill. Society for American Archaeology Memoirs 26.

Willey, P.
  1978 Preliminary Report of the Looted Human Skeletons from the Crow Creek Site (39BF11), South Dakota. Copy on file. Archaeology Laboratory, University of South Dakota.

  1981 Another View by One of the Crow Creek Researchers. Early Man 3(3):26.

Willey, P., and W.M. Bass
  1978 A Scalped Skull from Pawnee County. Kansas Anthropological Association Newsletter 24:1-11.

Willey, P., and T.E. Emerson
  ms The Osteology and Archaeology of the Crow Creek Massacre. Manuscript submitted for inclusion in Prehistory and Human Ecology of the Western Prairies and Northern Plains. J. Tiffany (ed.). Memoir of the Plains Anthropologist.

Willey, P., R.W. Mann, P.H. Moore-Jansen, R.L. Jantz, M. Guilbeau, and L. Meadows
  1987 Human Skeletal Material from the South Dakota Archaeological Research Center. Report for the State of South Dakota and the South Dakota Archaeological Research Center under Contract no. 87C-235.

Widdowson, E.M.
  1951 Mental Contentment and Physical Growth. The Lancet 260: 1316-1318.

Wilson, R.S.
  1976 Concordance in Physical Growth for Monozygotic and Dizygotic Twins. Annals of Human Biology 3:1-10.

Wood, W. Raymond (ed.)
  1976 Fay Tolton and the Initial Middle Missouri Variant. Missouri Archaeological Society Research Series 13.

Zimmerman, Larry J.
  ms Initial Coalescent Warfare and Its Impact on Extended Coalescent Settlement. Manuscript submitted for inclusion in Prehistory and Human Ecology of the Western Prairies and Northern Plains. J. Tiffany (ed.). Memoir of the Plains Anthropologist.

Zimmerman, L.J., and R. Alex
1981a How the Crow Creek Archaeologists View the Question of Reburial. Early Man 3(3):25-26.

1981b Digging Ancient Burials: The Crow Creek Experience. Early Man 3(3):3-10.

Zimmerman, L.J., T. Emerson, P. Willey, M. Swegle, J.B. Gregg, P. Gregg, E. White, C. Smith, T. Haberman, and M.P. Bumsted.
1981 The Crow Creek Site (39BF11) Massacre: A Preliminary Report. U.S. Corps of Engineers, Omaha District, Purchase Order DACW45-78-C-0018.

Zimmerman, L.J., and J.B. Gregg
1989 A History of the Reburial Issue in South Dakota. South Dakota Archaeology 13:89-100.

Zimmerman, L.J., J.B. Gregg, and P.S. Gregg
1980 Osteopathology in the Crow Creek Victims. Abstract of presented paper American Journal of Physical Anthropology 52(2):295.

Zimmerman, L.J., and R.G. Whitten
1980 Prehistoric Bones Tell a Grim Tale of Indian v. Indian. Smithsonian Magazine, September, pp. 100-107.

Zobeck, Terry Stewert
1983 Postcraniometric Variation among the Arikara. Ph.D. dissertation, University of Tennessee, Knoxville.